The Personal Digital Resilience Handbook

An essential guide to safe, secure and robust use of everyday technology

Dr David Wild

The Personal Digital Resilience Handbook:
An essential guide to safe, secure and robust use of everyday technology
mydigitalresilience.com

Copyright © 2020 by Dr. David Wild

ISBN: 978-0-578-79692-5

Project Editors:

All rights reserved. No part of this book may be reproduced in any form or by any electronic or mechanical means, including information storage and retrieval systems, without permission in writing from the author. The content of this book cannot be distributed, in any form, or offered as an electronic download, without permission from the author.

First Published: November 2020

The information in this book is distributed on an "As Is" basis, without warranty. The author has taken great care in preparation of this book, but assumes no responsibility for errors or omissions. No liability is assumed for incidental or consequential damages in connection with or arising out of the use of the information or programs contained herein.

Rather than use a trademark symbol with every occurrence of a trademarked name, this book uses the names only in an editorial fashion and to the benefit of the trademark owner, with no intention of infringement of the trademark.

Web addresses and menus selections are shown in bold. As shorthand, when describing navigation of menus on a computer to achieve a task, I will separate each part with a ">" symbol (arrow). For example, Apple menu > System Preferences > Users & Groups means to select the Apple menu, then select System Preferences, then select Users & Groups.

Contents

ABOUT THE AUTHOR & ACKNOWLEDGEMENTS

INTRODUCTION 1

CHAPTER 1: A DIGITALLY RESILIENT COMPUTER 5
   Consider a fresh start 5
   Compartmentalization...7
   Encryption and security 8
   Privacy and cloud sharing settings 10
   Sanitizing your computer 12
   Physical resilience...12

CHAPTER 2: A ROBUST DIGITAL BACKUP SYSTEM 15
   Backup technologies..15
   Backup strategy 1: cloud synchronization with offline backups 16
   Backup strategy 2: peer-to-peer synchronization with offline backups ..19
   Backup strategy 3: offline backups only 20
   Photos and videos..20
   Email backups 21
   Social media backups...22
   A critical family documents archive 22

CHAPTER 3: DIGITALLY RESILIENT INTERNET USE 25
   Reliable and redundant Internet access 25
   Secure your WiFi..26
   Lock down your browser..27
   Password and security management 28
   Protect your IP address with a VPN 33
   Evaluating online services for resilience...34
   Email strategy 35
   Avoiding phishing and ransomware attacks 38
   Masked credit cards 39
   Planting your flag 39
   Smart devices in your home 40

CHAPTER 4: A DIGITALLY RESILIENT SMARTPHONE..........................43
   Selecting a phone 43

Choosing the best cellular service.. 44
Switching to Voice-over-IP 45
Smartphone privacy & security settings 47
Smartphone backups & redundancy 48
Apps for resiliency 49

CHAPTER 5: ADVANCED DIGITAL RESILIENCE 53
Threat modeling 53
Using Linux and open-source software 55
An open source smartphone with GrapheneOS 57
Off-grid communications 58
Knowledge Reboot Kits 60
Deleting your digital trail 61

CHAPTER 6: CONCLUSION 65

About the Author

David Wild is Professor in the Luddy School of Informatics, Computing and Engineering at Indiana University where he researches and educates in crisis technologies, digital resilience, data science, data privacy, security and ethics, and biomedical data science. He is founder of the *Crisis Technologies Innovation Lab* that is researching and developing new digital technologies for the front line of emergency and disaster response.

Acknowledgements

I am indebted to Eva Galperin for introducing me to the term digital resilience, Michael Bazzell for not only the inspiration of his excellent books on privacy, but also his *This book was self-published* technical guide to self-publishing which provided the framework for publishing this book. I am not sure this book would have happened without that support. Thanks are due also to Sue Wild and Don Gregory for providing feedback on the first drafts of this book, and to my whole family and friends for consistent, loving support.

Introduction

I was first introduced to the term *digital resilience* in a breakfast meeting with Eva Galperin, Director of Cybersecurity at the Electronic Frontier Foundation (EFF). I was struggling to find a term for what I saw as an urgent and growing need for technology to be used in a different kind of way, a way that is more robust and reliable, and with more control over how we use it and what it does. I don't claim to have a monopoly over the use of the term, and others might use it differently, but I define digital resilience as *steps people and communities can take to make their use of digital technologies more robust and less prone to critical failure*. To the extent the term has been used, it has been mostly focused on business processes as an extension of cybersecurity. My interest, and the emphasis of this book, is in *personal* digital resilience, that is how we as individuals, families and communities can use technology in a way which mitigates the vulnerabilities and risks of using technology in the modern world.

Digital technology is incredibly powerful. The Internet has enabled a grand, global experiment in meeting our basic and advanced needs digitally instead of in more traditional corporeal ways. A massive, global infrastructure of compute servers and storage has been constructed by a relatively small number of companies like Google, Amazon and Microsoft, to power this experiment. Others such as Internet Service Providers and cellphone companies create the communications infrastructure to connect these servers to each other and to us. Service companies provide a treasure trove – or maybe a Pandora's Box – of applications layered onto this infrastructure. Food, clothing and lodging can now be purchased using a just-in-time logistics system that is itself dependent on the infrastructure; we get a job through LinkedIn, we Google our medical symptoms, we contact our neighbors on Facebook, and we obtain love and belonging on Tinder or Twitter, where we also gain or lose our self-esteem. The whole system – we might call it the Global Cloud – is now considered essential to our way of life. The Global Cloud has brought many benefits, such as enabling remote work, access to huge amounts of information, and convenient delivery of goods we might not be able to access locally. It has also brought problems, such as excluding those who do not have access to the necessary technologies, almost eliminating privacy, enabling cybercrime and state and corporate surveillance, and enabling monopoly corporations to undercut local businesses.

As I write this, we are in the midst of the global COVID19 pandemic. This has taken us to a level of critical dependency on the Global Cloud that would have seemed extraordinary less than a year ago. For many, it is now the primary source for meeting even basic needs, such as to interact with neighbors and colleagues for work or recreation, to get safety information important to our well-being, and to order goods. Both the benefits and problems of the Global Cloud are now amplified across the world. It is unclear how much this acceleration will persist once the pandemic is over, though it is likely that the Global Cloud will continue to grow unabated.

As well as being powerful, digital technology is also fragile, and this is a big concern given our dependence on it. Most of us are driving at 90mph down the digital freeway in cars that have no seat belts and with rusted axles that could break at any time. Barely a day goes by without a horrendous cyberattack that disables a corporation or a municipality appearing in the news. Until recently this was mainly from distributed denial-of-service (DDOS) attacks which would take a website or server offline for a few hours. Now we see much more devastating ransomware attacks where hackers take over and encrypt entire systems, demanding a ransom to decrypt them. As I write this a news story has just broken about a large national healthcare provider that is completely crippled by a ransomware attack, leaving it unable to run operations at its hospitals. These attacks happen to people like you and me too. Most of us know someone who has experienced a smaller-scale attack, maybe an identity theft or having an online account breached. Even when we are not under direct attack, we are under a kind of indirect attack on our brain. Companies collect huge amounts of data on us from the technology that we use, and they employ it to try to make us more valuable to them by modifying our behavior. This can take the form of selling our data to third parties, or using it to customize the content or advertisements we receive.

It's not just malicious or corporate actors that cause us problems. Technology breaks and fails in all kinds of interesting ways for often the smallest of reasons: a single downed power line brought down the entire North East U.S. power grid in 2003; a botched software update is regularly responsible for entire cloud systems going down. Computer components such as hard drives break often without warning. The impacts of climate change are amplifying our vulnerabilities to infrastructure failure. This year wildfires are ravaging across the western states of the U.S. Adding to the problems, winds are causing the Pacific Gas and Electricity company to impose rolling power blackouts due to the risk of starting new wildfires when power lines come down. Hurricanes and wildfires wipe out the critical infrastructure that the Global Cloud, and thus our lives, depend on. Cell phone towers fail, power and Internet access is lost. If we are lucky, they can be restored quickly. But other scenarios are worse: a cyberattack or solar weather event could disable key parts of the Global Cloud indefinitely; the companies we rely on could simply decide to withdraw services or be pressured to by an authoritarian government, which could also co-opt those services for mass surveillance. We thus have a new kind of vulnerability based on our dependence on the Global Cloud.

This book is a practical and detailed handbook for using digital technology in a way that will make you conscious of and responsive to these risks. By being digitally resilient you will be more safe, secure and private and will have control over your digital life. Chapters 1-4 give practical details about how to secure the important pieces of digital technology in your life like your computer and smartphone. At the end of each chapter is a checklist you can use to measure your progress. It is a check-up for all the digital technology in your life: we'll test the brakes and change the oil in your digital car, and install some seatbelts. Anyone can and should do these steps. Yes, that includes you, Uncle John and Aunt Maude. Kids can do these things too, with a bit of help, and if you are not comfortable doing these steps yourself, a tech-savvy grandchild or friend can likely help you out. Chapter 5 covers advanced digital resilience for those who want to take things further. The information described in this book is primarily for an audience in the United States, but many of the ideas are translatable to other countries.

Throughout the book, I will be anchoring on four basic concepts of digital resiliency. *Reliability and redundancy* is about understanding that any piece of technology will fail, and will sometimes fail spectacularly: as the adage goes, to err is human; to really screw things up requires a computer. Sometimes entire support systems will fail, such as in a power or Internet outage. Digitally resilient people bake this into their use of technology and have strengthened technologies and backup technologies in reserve ready to go. For this, adopt the survivalist's mantra "two is one, one is none": that is, if you have one of something it will break or be lost when you really need it, and then you will be in trouble; if you have two, then when one breaks you still have one. *Security* is about protecting the stuff that is most important to you from attack, from those with malicious intent. *Privacy* is about being able to make informed decisions about what happens with the streams of data that you generate every day, and how to keep information important to us from people you really don't want to have it. *Control* is about being able to make good decisions about who controls the things that are important to you. For example, if you have a stash of dollar bills under your mattress, you have full control of your money, but it may be at risk – from fire or theft. When you open a bank account you cede a lot of control to the bank, relying on them to keep an accurate tally of your balance, and enabling you to access your money through debit cards and ATMs. A bank account is more resilient in terms of security and robustness (in some ways), but less resilient in terms of control.

Digital resilience is not a static thing. The technology changes quickly and the things you need to do to be digitally resilient change too. As a reader of this book, you get access to a website at **https://mydigitalresilience.com** which has links to the resources mentioned in this book and product recommendations. I will keep these links and resources updated as things change including adding new content as needed.

I hope that you will share the information in this book with your family and friends. Why not give a copy as a Christmas or birthday present? You can make big improvements to the digital resilience of yourself and your loved ones. The next few years might well be quite rocky in many ways, from extreme weather events, fallout from the pandemic, political turbulence, cyberattack, and infrastructure failures. By being digitally resilient, you will be prepared and empowered.

Are you ready to be digitally resilient?

Chapter One

A Digitally Resilient Computer

Some of you might not even use a computer, relying on your smartphone or tablet for digital activity. But for most of us, one or more desktop or laptop computers, at home or at work, are a kind of Grand Central Station for our lives. The computer becomes a trusted friend that we go to when we want to research those strange symptoms we are having, send an email, figure out how to fix the toilet, write a document or sort out our finances on a spreadsheet. We keep important records in files on the hard disk or "in the Cloud".

Have you ever thought about just what could go wrong? What if your hard drive crashes and you lose all your files? What if you accidentally leave your laptop on a train or it is stolen from your bag? What if you go to the computer tomorrow morning and you see a red screen telling you that you are the victim of a ransomware attack? What if your health insurance company finds out you have been searching on a rare cancer and decides you are not worth covering? What if a hacker got access to that file with your social security number and bank details?

Worried yet? The good news is there are some simple and mostly completely free steps you can take that vastly reduce the risk of these things happening, and that reduce the impact if they do happen. In this chapter you will learn how to clean up your computer, decide if you wish to compartmentalize parts of your digital life, use disk encryption and secure passwords to make sure your files can never be accessed by anyone else, use better privacy and security settings, check for malware and delete unwanted programs, and keep your computer physically resilient. There is a lot to cover in this chapter, but if you take it step by step and follow the instructions carefully, you will then be the proud owner of a digitally resilient computer.

Even if you don't use a computer for most of your digital activities, be sure to read this chapter because it introduces come concepts like compartmentalization and encryption which are important for other parts of your digital life. If you follow the steps in this chapter, your computer will be hardened against accidental or malicious damage.

Consider a fresh start

Before you do anything else, I would like you to consider whether it is time for a fresh start. If you have had your current computer for years, and it feels clogged up and sluggish, this would be a great time to begin over and get a new one if you have the means to do so. There are many advantages to a fresh start on a new computer: you can run both in parallel for a while as you get the new one set up as you like it; you can be very deliberate about what you want to keep from your old computer and what you can get rid of; a new computer is likely to be faster, more reliable and less likely to break than your old one (for example, most new computers now have Solid State Drives – SSDs – that are much more reliable than traditional mechanical hard drives); you can keep your old computer as a backup (redundancy!). If you do buy a new computer, your choice is basically between a laptop or desktop machine and between Windows and MacOS (Apple) as the operating system. I am not going to get into a long discussion about Windows vs Mac here, except to say two things: I believe MacOS is generally more reliable and easier to set up than Windows, and is out of the box more secure and private. However, both can be made secure, and it really boils down to personal preference and budget. In this book I will show you how to achieve each step on both a Windows and a MacOS computer. Some of you might be aware that there are also two other options: Linux and Chromebooks. Linux is an open source operating system that can be installed in parallel with or as a replacement for Windows or MacOS on almost all machines. A discussion on Linux is out of scope for this book, but most of the measures described below will work similarly in Linux. Chromebooks are almost always laptop machines that are closely integrated with Google services and which run the Chrome operating system developed by Google. I am not going to cover Chromebooks here, but you can adapt some of the methods to Chromebooks. Note that usually Chromebooks automatically back your files up to Google Drive, and are considered quite secure (although not private, since Google gets to see everything) due to excellent Google security and malware protection. Therefore, Chromebooks do have some benefits for digital resilience out of the box.

Even if you are not in a position to buy a new computer, you can do a fresh start. Both Windows and MacOS let you wipe out your disk and reinstall the operating system "as new". Of course, this means that you may lose everything on your current computer, and so it is not something to be done lightly – for instance you would want to make sure you have followed the steps in the following chapter to back up your files before the reinstall. If you are ready to completely wipe your computer and start again, and are confident you have any important files backed up, here is how to do it.

Windows. I am going to assume you are using a version of Windows 10. To determine which version of Windows you are running, press the **Windows logo key** and **R** together, type **winver** in the Open box, and then select "OK". Windows 10 offers several options for reinstallation ranging from a lightweight "restore to what it was like when you got your PC and keep your files" through to a "wipe everything and start again"; older versions of Windows have some different options. All but one of these options requires you to create an installation medium, for instance on a USB flash drive. You then reboot your computer and boot from that medium to reinstall. Make sure you have access to the license key for Windows (lots of letters and numbers in blocks separated by dashes – this is likely in the documentation you got when you bought your computer). Some more recent machines automatically detect that you previously had a license installed, but you don't want to be in the position of having to buy a new license. Full instructions on how to reset or reinstall Windows 10 can be found here **https://support.microsoft.com/en-us/help/4000735/windows-10-reinstall**

MacOS. On MacOS machines, there is a built-in feature hidden away on a separate part of your drive called *MacOS Recovery* that lets you re-install the operating system. To access it, you will need to turn off your computer (**Apple Menu > Shutdown**), then turn on your computer while holding down a special key combination. There are three options for which sets of keys you hold down. If you hold down **Command (⌘)-R**, it will install the latest MacOS that was installed on your computer. This is usually the best option. Full stepwise instructions can be found on the Apple website at **https://support.apple.com/en-us/HT204904**. I recommend selecting "set up later" when asked to sign in with an Apple ID, and being sure to select a secure password (see section below). Also check custom settings so you can turn off sharing of analytics with Apple and make sure your time zone is correct.

If you decide not to do a fresh start, that is perfectly okay, and the way that you are going to set things up in the next chapter will make it much easier to move to a new machine or do a fresh install in the future if you wish.

Compartmentalization

Now is also a good time to decide if you want to *compartmentalize*. This is a way to protect different parts of your digital life from damage if there is a problem in one part, in much the same way that the hull of a ship is separated into sections so that if one compartment catches fire or hits an iceberg, the rest of the ship will stay afloat. Let's say you work for a large employer, who provides a laptop for you to use for your work. At home you connect to your work via a virtual private network (VPN), but you also use that same laptop for browsing the internet, checking your bank account, and storing your family photos. Imagine the company is hit with a ransomware attack which disables all machines on the company's network. In this scenario you have just lost access to all of your personal photos. Or in another scenario, maybe your company is sued and your laptop is seized as part of the investigation. Then all of your personal browsing history, bank details and photos will be accessible to the lawyers. Plus using a work computer for personal use might well be a violation of your employment terms. Even if something doesn't go seriously wrong, many employers install software on their computers that monitor how they are being used. If you had compartmentalized your work and personal computer use, your personal life would not be able to be impacted – at least at a technical level – by your work.

Work/personal is not the only way to compartmentalize. For example, you might want to have different members of your household use the same computer, or you might want to keep your hobbies separate from your family accounts. Interestingly, compartmentalization can be both a good and a bad thing for digital resilience. It can be good because it promotes security and privacy for different parts of your life; at the same time, by fully compartmentalizing you remove an opportunity for redundancy – for example being able to use your personal computer for work if your work machine breaks, and vice versa.

The most extreme form of compartmentalization is to have completely separate computers for different parts of your life. This is most common for work/personal separation and is usually appropriate, not least because it might be a violation of your contract to use a work computer for personal tasks. My recommendation is to keep work and personal activities on separate computers. Compartmentalization can also be achieved on a single computer in a variety of ways. For instance, you can create separate partitions of your hard disks with completely different instances of the operating system, so the computer is effectively working as two machines in one, although without the benefit of redundancy of hardware (for instance if the hard disk dies, both compartments are toast). In this instance the computer is "dual boot" and you can boot up to either operating system. This is quite complex to implement, and has some risks, so I don't normally recommend it unless you are very technically adept. Easier is to have different *user accounts* on your computer for different compartments.

This doesn't offer full separation, but enables you to have some division, at least preventing you from accidentally sharing your personal browsing history on a work video call.

Windows. To set up users on Windows, go to **Settings > Accounts**. Windows offers two ways to manage users: using Microsoft Live online accounts, or local accounts on this PC. I always recommend using local accounts only. To stop using a Live account and instead start using a local account, click on **Your Info** in the Accounts page and choose Sign in with a local account. To add an additional account, in the Accounts page click on **Family & Other Users**, then click the link to add a user to this PC.

MacOS. On MacOS, you can set up additional users from **Apple Menu > System Preferences > Users & Groups**. You will then be able to switch users by clicking on the menu bar at the top right of the screen and selecting a different user.

Encryption and security

Encryption is a way to encode your data so that it is difficult or impossible for someone to access it without your password. Having strong encryption and security settings on your machine is essential in ensuring that only the people that you want to physically access the contents of your computer will be able to do so. If you have encryption and strong security set up, then even if your laptop is stolen on the bus, or a curious child decides to mess with your desktop machine when you are gone, then none of your valuable data and files will be accessible to them. In this section, you will learn how to increase security and privacy by encrypting your computer's disk and protected by a strong password. You will do this in a way which maximizes your control over access to the contents of your disk.

First, make sure that you have a system of strong passwords for unlocking your computer. Depending on what kind of computer you have and how it is set up, you might need just one password, or you might need two: one for unlocking your account and one for decrypting your disk when you turn on the computer. As will be described later, you can do away with the bother of remembering passwords for other uses like online accounts by employing a password manager, but the password that unlocks your computer you will need to remember. For a password to be secure, it should be long (more than 8 characters, preferably longer), and not something that you could find in a dictionary. It is not considered necessary to change your password periodically unless you believe it may have been compromised. My recommendation is to pick a three- or four-word phrase that means something to you but wouldn't be guessable by someone who knows you, and use that as your password. For example, if you have a dog named Fido who loves playing catch, your password could be "fidolovesplayingcatch" or "fido loves playing catch". If you want to make it even more secure, you can add some related numbers – for example if Fido was born in 2020, your password could be "fidolovesplayingcatch2020". An alternative is to think of a long phrase, and then use the initial letters as your password. For example, maybe Fido loves playing catch in the park at night. Your password could be the first letters of that phrase, maybe with 2020 added: "flpcitpan2020". The point is you can make a secure password that is complex but easy to remember because it is derived from a meaningful phrase for you. I don't recommend using a password that you have used previously particularly for any online accounts, as it might already have been breached and be in lists of passwords known to hackers (if you want to check this, go to **https://haveibeenpwned.com/Passwords**). Should you write down your password somewhere in case you forget it? That is your decision, but if you do, make sure to keep that piece of paper with the password on it somewhere secure, maybe in a safe.

Windows. To change your account password in Windows, I will assume that you have followed the earlier advice and you have a local account on your computer, and are not signing in using a Live account. Go to **Settings > Accounts**, then click on "Sign-in options" in the panel at the left. Choose the "Password" option, then click "Change" to change your password to your new, secure password. You will notice that Windows now gives you lots of options for how to sign in, like PINs and picture passwords. I do not recommend you use any of those: stick with your secure password. While you are here, make sure that the require sign-in option is set to "When PC wakes up from sleep", and that both options in the Privacy section are set to off. Once you have done this, you will need to check the settings for when Windows requires you to enter the password. Go to **Settings > Personalization > Lock Screen > Screen Saver Settings**. Choose the screen saver you want (such as Blank), then decide how long you want the computer to remain idle before the screen saver comes on and the computer locks. Make sure the box "On resume, display logon screen" is checked, and then click OK. Now, the computer will require you to type your password once it has been idle for the time you set in the box.

MacOS. To change your local account password on MacOS, Go to **Apple > System Preferences > Users & Groups**. You should see your account listed along with any other accounts that have been created on your machine. Click on the **Change Password** button to change your password. Make sure that each account has a strong password.

Now that you have your accounts protected with a strong password, you will need to make sure the disk is encrypted. On Windows, you can do this with Device Encryption or Bitlocker. On MacOS, the built-in encryption system is called FileVault.

Windows. Microsoft makes things somewhat confusing by having two methods to encrypt your disk. Windows 10 has a built-in encryption system called Device Encryption. This works on all versions of Windows 10, but has some hardware requirements: your computer must have a Trusted Platform Module and UEFI boot enabled. You can tell if Device Encryption is available on your machine by going to **Settings > Update & Security**. If you see "Device Encryption" in the panel on the left, you are in luck. Click Turn On to begin the process of encrypting your disk. You will be prompted to save a copy of a recovery key that you can use if you lose your password. I recommend saving this to a USB flash drive stored in a secure location. If you do not meet the hardware requirements for Device Encryption, but are running Windows Pro, you can use a built-in program called Bitlocker to encrypt your disk. More information on both of these can be found on the Microsoft website at **https://support.microsoft.com/en-us/help/4028713/windows-10-turn-on-device-encryption**. If your computer is not compatible with either method, you can still use VeraCrypt (see below).

MacOS. When you first set up your MacOS computer, you are given the option to turn on FileVault encryption. To check whether it is enabled on your computer, go to **Apple > System Preferences > Security & Privacy**. Tap on the "FileVault" tab, and if it is already enabled it will show "Filevault is turned on". If it is not, follow the instructions at **https://support.apple.com/en-us/HT204837** to turn it on. You will be given two options for unlocking your disk if you forget your password: unlocking through iCloud or creating a local recovery key. I strongly recommend creating a local recovery key and storing it in a safe place, rather than unlocking through iCloud, which would mean that if your iCloud account is breached someone could unlock your disk. Once you have enabled FileVault, MacOS will begin to encrypt the contents of your hard disk in the background, so long as you are plugged into the power supply. You can still use the computer during encryption and can check progress of the encryption in the FileVault tab.

If you have sensitive files that require some extra security – maybe containing passwords or PIN numbers – then consider using an encrypted container on your drive. I recommend VeraCrypt (**https://www.veracrypt.fr**). Using an encrypted container means that the files in it are "double encrypted" – the container contents are encrypted with one password, and the container itself resides on an encrypted hard disk. VeraCrypt is fairly simple to use and works on all platforms. If you have a second drive or a USB flash drive, you can also encrypt it entirely. If your Windows machine is not compatible with device encryption and Bitlocker, VeraCrypt is your best option to encrypt at least some of your files.

Privacy and cloud sharing settings

Out of the box, both Windows and MacOS computers send quite a bit of information back to Microsoft and Apple respectively, and the manufacturers increasingly assume that you are comfortable sharing your files, photos and settings with them for the benefit of synchronization between devices and cloud storage for backup. By changing your privacy and cloud sharing settings, you can vastly reduce the amount of information that is sent out about you and you make informed decisions about what to share. In making these changes you will improve your digital resilience by increasing the control you have over your computer and the data that is transmitted about you, as well as increasing your privacy. First, let's change some basic privacy settings.

Windows. On Windows, I will again assume you are using a local account, not logging in with a Microsoft Live account – if you haven't made that change yet, now is the time to do it (**Settings > Accounts > Your info > Sign in with a local account**). Most of the privacy settings can be found in the Privacy section of Windows settings. Make sure everything is turned off in the "General, Speech and Inking" & "Typing personalization" tabs. Under "Diagnostics & feedback", choose "Required diagnostic data" for the first option, then turn everything else off. When you get to the bottom, click the button to delete diagnostic data that Microsoft has collected. Under "Activity history", make sure everything is unchecked. Once you have done this, go through each of the categories for App permissions and turn off everything that is not essential for the work you want to do with the computer. In particular, you should make sure that location is turned off, and only essential apps have access to the camera and microphone. Once you have done that, go to **Settings > System > Notifications & actions** and turn off "Show notifications on the lock screen". This will ensure that no one can see notifications on your screen when the computer is locked. Finally, I suggest you get rid of Cortana, Microsoft's voice command software. Click on the Windows menu, scroll down until you see Cortana, then right click and select **More > App settings**. Turn all app permissions off, then click the button to terminate the app. Once you have done this, click the button to uninstall Cortana.

MacOS. On MacOS, I will assume that you have the most up to date version of the operating system (currently Catalina). Go into **Apple Menu > System Preferences > Security & Privacy** and click on the "Privacy" tab. Click down each of the categories like location services and contacts, and see which applications have requested access to that category of services. You can then uncheck any apps you do not want to have access to those services. Unless you have pressing need for it, I strongly recommend that you turn off location services altogether – there are very few reasons your computer needs to know your location. Be very selective about which applications can access your camera and microphone, and remember that you can always re-enable any applications in the future. No routine applications should be granted full disk access. Catalina gives you control over which files and folders are available to applications at the folder level, so work through carefully each application and ensure that they only have access to the folders that are really needed. Select "Limit Ad Tracking" in the Advertising category and press the button to Reset Advertising Identifier. Finally ensure that all options are unchecked in the "Analytics & Improvements" category.

The next step is to take a look at the cloud settings for your computer. Both Apple and Microsoft provide an online "cloud" backup service that can store your files on remote server machines. The Apple cloud is called iCloud, and the Microsoft cloud is called OneDrive. Both services are quite similar. They offer 5GB of free online storage, with additional storage available with paid plans. Data is encrypted in transit (i.e. while being communicated between your computer and the remote file servers) and at rest (when they are stored on the remote servers) but the encryption is controlled by the company, so Apple or Microsoft is able to unencrypt your files for whatever purposes they desire. Cloud storage is good for digital resilience, in that it improves redundancy by ensuring that files on your computer are backed up; but in this case the benefit is balanced by a reduction in control and privacy, because someone else now has access to your files. In the next chapter, I describe a robust, private system for backups that is fully under your control. For this reason, I think the best approach is to turn off all iCloud or OneDrive services. If you already rely on one of these services, you should wait until you have implemented the steps in the next chapter before turning them off. However, turning them off does come at a cost. If you want to keep having your photos, messages and other information synchronized between your devices, you will have to accept a system that is not quite so smooth. If you want to see some of the risks of using these services, try searching for "iCloud photos leak" on Google. Ultimately the decision is up to you. If you decide to keep using iCloud or OneDrive, at least ensure that you understand what you are sharing with these services.

Windows. If OneDrive is running on your computer, you will see a small blue cloud in the Taskbar usually at the bottom right (you might need to click on the ^ symbol to see this). To turn off OneDrive, open OneDrive, select **Help & Settings > Settings**, then on the Account tab click "Unlink this PC" and then "Unlink Account". Some versions of Windows allow you to fully uninstall the OneDrive app by clicking on the Windows menu then right clicking on the OneDrive app, and selecting "Uninstall". If you wish to delete any files that have been previously uploaded to OneDrive, go to the OneDrive website at **https://onedrive.live.com** and log in with your Microsoft Live account details: you may wish to wait until you have implemented the backup strategy described in the next chapter before doing this.

MacOS. On MacOS, you likely created an Apple ID when you set up your computer for the first time, or maybe you use an Apple ID previously created for a phone. If you did a fresh start, you hopefully followed my recommendation to skip entering an Apple ID. If you are logged into an Apple account, you can completely sign out of your Apple ID on your computer. This will automatically disable iCloud. It will mean that you will no longer get app updates from the App Store, but you can always periodically sign into the App Store to look for updates and then sign out again. Most applications can be download from the provider's website without need to use the Apple store. First let's check what is currently being shared with iCloud. Go to **Apple Menu > System Preferences**. If you see a message at the top saying "Sign in to your Apple ID", you are already signed out. If you see your account ID and picture, click to access your Apple account information. Click on "iCloud" in the left pane and then select which kinds of information you want to share with iCloud – or turn them all off if you are ready to stop using iCloud altogether. When you turn off iCloud Drive (file sharing) be sure to click to keep a copy of your files on your local machine. Once you have done this, you can sign out of your Apple ID at the bottom left of the same window. Once you have completed this, and have implemented the backup strategy described in the next chapter, you should log into your iCloud account at **https://icloud.com** and delete all the content you no longer wish to be shared with Apple.

Sanitizing your computer

Your computer is almost digitally resilient, but you need to do a bit of spring cleaning to make sure that there is nothing lurking on it that could compromise your resiliency. If you have had your computer for a while, and didn't do a fresh start, I would begin by installing and running the Malwarebytes program (**https://www.malwarebytes.com**) to check for malware. You don't need the paid version, simply do a single scan and make sure that anything that is "quarantined" is selected for removal. I recommend running Malwarebytes around once a month – if you have good Internet hygiene (see the chapter on Internet use) and avoid clicking on links in emails and going to untrusted websites, you are likely to avoid the kinds of malware and trackers that Malwarebytes searches for. For Windows computers, I do recommend an antivirus also – my preferred is the ClamAV open source antivirus (**http://www.clamav.net/**).

Physical resilience

The final piece of the puzzle is physical resilience. This means preventing your computer from becoming damaged, stolen or accessed without your consent, as well as being able to use your computer in an adverse environment, such as during a power outage, or on the floor in the corner of a far-away airport.

More than anything, ensure that your computer is secured with a strong password, and that notifications are turned off on the screen when the computer is locked, as described earlier. A desktop computer should be kept in a location that can be secured such as with a locked door, and be kept at least a few inches off the floor in case you experience a flood. Also ensure it cannot easily be knocked over, and is well away from coffee spillage. For around $100, you can buy an Uninterruptable Power Supply (UPS) that will ensure that your desktop computer will keep running in a power outage for enough time for you to finish up what you are doing and do an orderly shutdown of the computer.

For a laptop, it is worth investing in a good laptop bag with plenty of padding, and preferably with the ability to lock the laptop portion of the bag. Always try to keep your laptop in your possession when traveling. If you travel a lot with a laptop, I think it is worth investing in some accessories to increase your resilience while away from home. I recommend having a pouch in your backpack containing a spare power adapter, a power bank with at least 20,000 mAh capacity that you can use to recharge your computer as well as your smartphone, plus whatever collection of cables you might need.

If your computer has a webcam, I strongly recommend covering the lens when you are not using it, to remove any risk of someone accessing your webcam maliciously. Some cameras now have built in covers that can be flipped open and shut. If you do not have one of these, I recommend the camera covers from Silent Pocket (**https://silent-pocket.com/products/webcam-cover**) – or you can just use some tape or a label. Similarly, if your computer has a microphone, disconnect it when not in use if it is an external microphone; for internal microphones, I recommend using a MicLock (**https://mic-lock.com**) to reduce the risk of inadvertent recording of sound.

Digitally Resilient Computer Checklist

- [ ] Decide a fresh start strategy (new computer, operating system reset, or none)
- [ ] Make any backups needed and implement your fresh start strategy
- [ ] Decide on a compartmentalization strategy
- [ ] Create any additional accounts needed for your compartmentalization strategy
- [ ] Ensure all accounts have a secure password (>8 characters, not in dictionary)
- [ ] Encrypt the disk if possible
- [ ] Create VeraCrypt containers for any particularly sensitive files
- [ ] Review privacy and cloud storage settings in your operating system
- [ ] Run Malwarebytes and install antivirus if using Windows
- [ ] Make sure computer is kept in a physically secure environment
- [ ] Consider a UPS for desktop machines and a spare power bank for laptops
- [ ] Create a laptop travel kit with extra cables, power supplies, etc.
- [ ] Secure computer webcams and microphones

Chapter Two

A Robust Digital Backup System

In this chapter, I will describe how to keep your important files safe. This is done by creating *backups*, or extra copies of your files, so that if something goes wrong with one copy you still have others to fall back on. I will introduce four technologies for backups: *cloud synchronization, peer-to-peer synchronization, portable SSD drives,* and *USB flash drives,* and then show how these can be used in three different backup strategies. Note that this backup system is just for your files, not for everything else on your computer like your settings and applications. While "full disk backups" are available, I don't personally find them useful, as it is usually easy to rebuild them if you need to on a new computer, and I always prefer a fresh start when I get a new computer. I will also show you how to create a *critical family documents* archive that contains your most important identity, financial and other documents.

Once you complete the steps in this chapter, you will have a backup strategy that will keep your files safe and secure. I recently suffered a hard disk failure on one of my desktop machines, and within 6 hours I had visited Best Buy, bought a $200 SSD drive, fully restored my important programs and files and was back up and back to working as if nothing has happened. This was only possible because I had implemented one of the backup strategies described in this chapter.

Backup technologies

Cloud synchronization is usually the most convenient method for backing up files, and is a natural option if you need to have multiple devices access the same files. Cloud synchronization works by automatically copying your files onto one or more remote servers. When you update a file on one computer, it will be immediately copied to the cloud server (assuming you have Internet access – if not, it will be copied once you reconnect), and subsequently automatically copied from the cloud server to all other devices you have decided to synchronize with. Most services also offer the ability to share files with other people, and some allow people to work collaboratively on the same files at the same time.

The most common cloud synchronization services are iCloud (included with Apple products), OneDrive (included with Microsoft products), DropBox, Box, and Google Drive. All of these services suffer from a serious flaw in the way that they handle encryption (see the previous chapter for a discussion on encryption). They do encrypt your files in transit (i.e. while being copied from your devices to the remote servers), and at rest (i.e., in storage on the remote server), and they offer advanced password security through two-factor authentication (see next chapter). However, the encryption uses keys that are managed by the company. This means that not only will your files be exposed if your password is breached, but they can also be accessed by employees of the company, and if the encryption keys are breached, all of your files could be available to anyone with the keys.

For this reason, I recommend selecting a cloud synchronization service that is *zero knowledge, end-to-end encrypted*. Zero knowledge means that the company has no way to access the content of your files; end to end encryption means that the encryption happens on your devices, not on the remote servers, and the encryption keys are held locally. Three popular services that meet this requirement are Sync, Tresorit, and SpiderOak. Sync (**https://sync.com**) is the lowest cost of the three, offering up to 5GB of storage for free, and 2TB for $8/month. The Tresorit Business Plus plan (**https://tresorit.com/subscribe-business-plus-trial**) costs $20/month for 2TB, while the SpiderOak OneBackup plan (**https://spideroak.com/one**) costs $14/month for 2TB. SpiderOak and Tresorit provide Windows, Mac, Linux, Android and iOS apps that automatically synchronize files for you. Sync provides Windows, Mac, Android and iOS apps, but does not work on Linux. Of critical importance, all of these services include *versioning* of files. This means that you can "wind back the clock" and access files as they used to be at some point in the past (the extent to which you can wind back depends on the service, for example Sync.com Pro Solo allows 180 days). This is hugely important in protecting against ransomware attacks. If you are the victim of a ransomware attack, all of your files on your machine will be encrypted by someone else's keys, and you will be unable to access them. If you are using cloud synchronization, this means that the copies on the remote server and other devices will also be updated to the maliciously encrypted files. Versioning allows you to go back and recover a version of your files before the ransomware took effect.

An alternative to cloud synchronization is peer-to-peer synchronization, where files are not stored on a remote server, but are simply synchronized directly between devices that you control. The most commonly used software is called Syncthing (**https://syncthing.net**). This is completely free and open source, and apps are available for Windows, MacOS, Linux and Android, but not iOS. You can choose whether to only synchronize files when devices are on the same network, such as your home router, or whether to allow synchronization between networks such as when you are traveling, in which case some remote servers are used for the purpose of keeping track of the IP addresses of the devices that are synchronizing. I have found Syncthing to be reliable, but the lack of synchronization of files to remote servers means that the only backups are on the devices that you own. Syncthing does offer some level of versioning, but it is not enabled by default. Generally, the advantages of peer-to-peer synchronization are that it is free, and you are not putting your files on any computers other than the ones that you own. The disadvantage is that the lack of remote backup reduces your resilience, as if all your devices become inoperable you have lost your files. However, with a good offline backup strategy as described below, this can be a good and free option.

Portable SSD drives offer a way to do backups locally onto storage that you own and control. SSD drives are much faster and more reliable than the older mechanical hard disks, and a 1TB external drive that plugs into a USB port can now be purchased for around $200. Using the same technology, USB flash drives offer a very compact way to backup files, and you can now buy a 256GB USB flash drive for about $30.

Backup strategy 1: cloud synchronization with offline backups

This strategy will rely heavily on cloud synchronization with versioning, using periodic offline backups in case of failure of the cloud synchronization service. This is likely to be the most appropriate strategy for most people, and will provide for secure, robust, and redundant backups.

I will use the Sync Pro Solo cloud service, which will cost $8/month, offering 2GB of storage, zero knowledge end-to-end encryption, and 180 days of versioning included. Go to **https://sync.com** and sign up for this service If you wish to try it out for free first, you can begin with the free 5GB plan and then upgrade later. Make sure to enable two-factor authentication (see next chapter for how to do this). Once your account is set up, download the appropriate app from **https://www.sync.com/install/** and follow the instructions at **https://www.sync.com/help/the-sync-desktop-application/#syncinstall**. Once the app is set up, you will have a folder called Sync on your computer. Anything that is moved into or saved in the Sync folder will be synchronized with the remote server and any other devices that you are using. I suggest testing this by creating a small "test" file with a text editor or Microsoft Word, and saving it in the Sync folder. You should see the small Sync icon show a spinning wheel as it is uploading, then a check mark once it is uploaded. Then go to the web panel on the Sync.com website and you should see the file there. The Sync folder is now your main location for your documents. I recommend taking the opportunity to sort through your files, do some spring cleaning, and put all of your important files into the Sync folder. You can then follow the same process to set up Sync on another device, and can also access your files by logging into the Sync.com website to ensure that they have uploaded.

You now have a good backup system with remote storage and versioning. However, it is important to have offline backups in case something goes wrong with the Sync system. In this instance I recommend making offline backups at least once a quarter, and monthly if you have the time. Based on your storage requirements, you could use either an external SSD drive or a USB flash drive, or both, for offline storage. My recommendation for most people is to use an SSD drive with at least 1TB. It is important that you use encryption on the drive, so that if you lose it or it is stolen, no-one will have access to your files.

To setup an encrypted SSD or flash drive, first ensure that VeraCrypt is installed on your computer (**https://www.veracrypt.fr/code/VeraCrypt/**). On a MacOS or Windows machine, you will also need to make sure that you are logged in with an account that has administrator privileges (if you only have one account, then this will be the case). Insert the drive into the USB port of the computer, and then open up VeraCrypt (see opening screen in Figure 2.1). Click on "Create Volume", then choose the second option, "Encrypt a non-system partition/drive" and choose "Standard VeraCrypt volume". Now choose "Select Device…" and look for your USB or SSD device listed. Be careful to identify the correct device for your USB or SSD drive by the name or the size. On a Linux machine, it will likely be called something like **/dev/sdb**; on MacOS it will be called something like **/dev/rdiskX** and on a Windows machine **Removable Disk X**. Under the device name you will see a list of partitions: if it is a new device, there is usually just one partition. Select the partition and click OK (be careful not to select your hard drive partition!) Select "Create encrypted volume and format it", click "Next" on the encryption options, "Next" again to confirm. Now create a secure password for the drive (see discussion in last chapter on selecting a secure password). On the next screen, answer if you want to be able to store files larger than 4GB (usually no), then on the final screen wiggle your mouse a bit to improve the randomness of the encryption, then click Format, and wait for the formatting to complete. Congratulations, you now have a fully encrypted backup drive!

Whenever you want to use your encrypted drive, insert the drive into the USB port. On MacOS, when you insert the drive, you will get a message that "the disk you inserted was not readable by this computer". Just click Ignore – it cannot be read because it is encrypted. Now open up VeraCrypt, click "Select Device…" and select the partition that you formatted. Then click "Mount", type the secure password, and you will be able to access the drive. On Windows, it will be given a drive letter – click on the **Files icon > This PC > Devices and drives > (whatever drive letter was used)**. On MacOS, open the Finder window, and under Locations you should see your drive with the name "NO NAME". To create an offline backup your files, go to the file folder you want to copy – for example the Sync folder, right click on the folder (Control-click on MacOS), select Copy, then navigate to the backup drive, right/control click, and select Paste. Once the folder has copied, I recommend renaming it with the date it was copied in YYYY-MM-DD format, e.g. Sync 2020-10-09. You can then keep multiple backups on the disk until you run out of space, at which point delete the oldest backup. Once you have created an offline backup on your backup drive, eject it, and put it in a secure place such as a fire safe until your next backup.

There is one more step I recommend: download the VeraCrypt installation files for Windows, Mac and Linux from **https://www.veracrypt.fr/en/Downloads.html**. Copy the installation files onto a separate, unencrypted USB flash drive (a cheap 8GB drive should suffice). This means if you ever need to access the files on your backup drive using a machine that doesn't have VeraCrypt, you have it ready to install. It also means that if the VeraCrypt website ever goes away, you still can install it on a computer. Update the installation files periodically, and keep the VeraCrypt installation USB flash drive in the secure location with your backup drive.

Figure 2.1. Opening screen for VeraCrypt on MacOS.

Backup strategy 2: peer-to-peer synchronization with offline backups

This strategy is identical to the previous strategy, except that instead of using a cloud synchronization service, you will use Syncthing for peer-to-peer synchronization. You might wish to choose this option if you have several computers that you want to sync your files between, and you either want to save the cost of the cloud service, or you are not comfortable with having your files stored on remote servers (even encrypted).

To set up Syncthing, go to **https://syncthing.net/downloads/** and download and install the appropriate application on each machine you want to use for file synchronization. For Windows, this will be the SyncTrayzor bundle, with the SyncTrayzorSetup-x64.exe likely the correct installation file to download. For MacOS use the syncthing-macos bundle and download the dmg installation file. Then follow the setup instructions at **https://docs.syncthing.net/intro/getting-started.html**. When you run Syncthing on Windows or MacOS you should see the Syncthing icon that looks a bit like a steering wheel in the toolbar. If you click "Open" you will be taken to the local Syncthing webpage (or you can go directly in the browser to **http://127.0.0.1:8384**). Each device is identified by a 56-character device ID, which needs to be typed into the other computers that you are sharing with – or you can use a QR code if the computer has a camera. If you have two machines sharing, each will need to separately authorize the other machine. On one machine, go to **Actions > Show ID**, and then on the other go to Remote Devices on the main page and click on **+ Add Remote Device**. If both machines are on the same network, it will likely give you the option to select the ID for the device – make sure it is the same one shown on the first machine, and give the device a name that is meaningful to you. You can follow the same procedure the other way round – the first device will in a short time automatically ask you if you want to reciprocally add the second device. If you have more devices to add, you will need to add each of them into the "cluster" of synchronized computers.

Now set up a folder to synchronize files. Choose one machine as a primary. On the primary machine, open the Syncthing local webpage. On the left side, you can see folders that are shared. There is a default folder already set up, but not yet shared. I prefer to create a new folder – called Syncthing – instead of using this default. This is partly because the default Syncthing folder is called "Sync" just the same as Sync.com, so if you ever want to have both on the same machine, you would not really want to be using the same folder. So let's first delete the default folder (**Default Folder > Edit > Remove**). Then click the button to add a folder, and select the name of a folder you want to use for your files. Enter this under "Folder Label". The path to the folder will be shown in the third box. Once you have done this, click on the Sharing tab and make sure to check the box for all the devices in your cluster. After a few minutes, you should see a message pop up on the Syncthing local webpage asking if you want to add the folder that you just shared. Click "Add", then click the Sharing tab to make sure all devices are selected for sharing, then click "Save". Now you are done! Create a test file as described in the first strategy and make sure it gets synchronized between devices – this may take a few minutes.

You are now ready to start copying files into your Syncthing folder, in just the same way as you do with cloud synchronization. Because Syncthing does not store files on remote servers, and doesn't have the same versioning capabilities as Sync and other cloud synchronization services, I recommend you follow the same offline backup strategy as previously described, but make backups at least once a month, and weekly if possible.

Backup strategy 3: offline backups only

A third strategy is offline backups only. You would use this strategy if you only have one computer, thus have no need to share files between computers, and if you either don't want to pay for cloud synchronization or are not comfortable having your files stored in the cloud, even encrypted. If you are only using offline backups, I recommend that you have two SSD drives that you alternate to use for backups, so that you have some extra redundancy, and ensure that you keep one of them in a different location to the other, preferably outside your house. You will likely want to back up at least once a week.

Photos and videos

Photos and videos pose some special challenges for backups, mainly because they use a lot of storage, and also because they tend to be handled in special ways by computer operating systems. I am going to make some recommendations below for how to handle photos.

Windows. On Windows, you most likely have your photos stored in a folder called Pictures, and use the built-in application called Photos to access them. If you want to keep all of your folders backed up using cloud or peer-to-peer synchronization you will need to instead make a new folder (you can still call it "Pictures") inside your synchronized folder (e.g. Sync or Syncthing). Once you have done this, open two windows, open your current Pictures folder, select all the files or folders, and drag them into the synchronization pictures folder you just made. Now set up the Photo application to use this folder instead of the old one. Open the Photos application, click on the "…" at the top right to access the menu, then click the button to add a folder. Select the new pictures folder, and once you have done that remove the old one. You are now set up so that all your pictures will be backed up.

A problem with this strategy comes if you have so many gigabytes of photos that it exceeds the space that you have in a cloud synchronization service. It may also take many hours to copy across the files. You might thus consider only copying across more recent photos (maybe the last couple of years) to the cloud synchronization, then leaving the older pictures in the main Pictures folder, and using an offline backup strategy for the older photos. If you do this, make sure when you add new photos that they go into the new, synchronized pictures folder and not the old one.

MacOS. If you use Apple devices, the default is to use their ecosystem for managing photos, including the MacOS Photos app. The problem with this is that it locks you into the Apple ecosystem, so it is then difficult to access your photos on anything other than an Apple device. Unlike Windows, photos are not stored in a standard way, but are kept in a proprietary database format. However, it is very difficult to manage photos well on a MacOS without being in this ecosystem. Therefore for MacOS users, I recommend a strategy where you use the Apple Photos ecosystem to manage your photos, but you use the Export function to save a second copy of your photos in standard formats in a folder that is backed up. So in a similar way to Windows, create a new folder (let's say it's "Pictures") in your synchronized / backed up folder. The first time you do this, go into the Photos application, and go to

Edit > Select All to select all of your photos. Now go to **File > Export > Export unmodified original for X items**, and click Export. You will then be asked to select a folder – select the new Pictures folder. Exporting will likely take a long time, and it will take a long time to synchronize if you are using a cloud service, so be patient. Once this is done, the process is much easier. Every time you import new photos, make sure the newly imported photos are selected, then follow the same process as just described to export. You now have a backup of all your photos in standard format. If you ever want to rebuild your Apple photos database, you can simply import them back in.

Email backups

You probably use an email provider like Gmail for your email. Maybe you have multiple accounts. These services tend to be very reliable, so we don't think much about what would happen if we lost access. But it could happen – maybe your email account gets suspended for some reason by Google; or you accidentally delete all your old emails; or your email provider just decides to stop providing service one day. So it is very important to keep backups of your email that you control. The easiest way to do this is with a program called *Thunderbird* (**https://www.thunderbird.net**). Thunderbird is a free and open source email client for your computer. It's a bit clunky, so you might not want to use it for actually writing and reading emails. I will describe how to use it for backups. Download the application from the Thunderbird website. Open Thunderbird and go to **Tools > Account Settings > Account Actions > Add Mail Account...** Enter your email account details. If you use a common service like Gmail, it will automatically figure out the right settings, but if you use a less common email provider, you may need to enter the server settings manually. Do this for all of the email accounts you want to keep backed up. If you are using Thunderbird just for backup purposes, you probably want to turn off notifications of new email. To do this on Windows, in Thunderbird go to **Options > General > When new messages arrive:** Uncheck "Show an alert". Uncheck "Play a sound". On MacOS, go to **System Preferences > Notifications** and select Thunderbird, and turn notifications off. You can now leave the Thunderbird application running in the background and all your email will be saved to a local file.

This already has vastly improved your email resilience – you have a local backup on your computer as well as on Gmail or whatever service you use. But you probably want to back up your email offline or using synchronization. To do this, make a copy of the Thunderbird email folder and put it either on a backup SSD or in your synchronization folder. I suggest making a folder called "Email backup" and put a recent copy of the installation file for Thunderbird (maybe for multiple platforms) into that folder. You should also copy the Thunderbird email file into that folder. This means that if you ever want to rebuild your email, you have a copy of the Thunderbird installation file as well as your Thunderbird email database. The Thunderbird folder is called "Profiles" and you can copy it anywhere using cut and paste. On Windows, the folder is at **C:\Users\<Windows user name>\AppData\Roaming\Thunderbird**. On MacOS, it is stored in **~/Library/Thunderbird** (you can get there with **Go > Home**, then select "Library" and "Thunderbird"). To restore, install Thunderbird, delete the Profiles file in the new Thunderbird instance, and replace it with the one that has been backed up.

Social media backups

Most people don't think about social media when considering backups. Depending on how you use different social media services, there may or may not be valuable content in your posts and interactions with others that you want to preserve. Backing up your social media accounts means that your content could potentially outlive the platform. Facebook allows you to download your data relatively easily, with options for format (HTML or JSON), picture quality and date range: follow the instructions at **https://www.facebook.com/help/1701730696756992** to download your data. On Twitter, you can request your tweet archive in Settings – see **https://help.twitter.com/en/managing-your-account/how-to-download-your-twitter-archive** for more information. Instagram has a data download tool – you can learn more at **https://help.instagram.com/contact/505535973176353**. Once you have downloaded your data, move it into your synchronization or documents folder to ensure it gets backed up.

A critical family documents archive

In addition to backing up your existing files, I suggest also creating a *critical family documents archive*. This is an electronic copy of "critical family documents" – that is, those documents which are essential for proving your identity, ownership of property, and so on. Often, we have these documents scattered around in paper form. A digitally resilient strategy is to create mirror image electronic and paper copies.

To create the archive, first create a new folder in your documents / synchronization folder, say called Critical Family Documents. Here you will assemble all of your critical documents. If they don't already exist in electronic form, you will need to scan them (most printers also work as scanners nowadays). What you put into this archive is up to you, but here is what I keep:

Accounts and Passwords: Copies of password manager files (see next chapter), two factor authentication backup codes, and any other account information documents.

Financial and Property: Copies of home and car title deeds, mortgage documents, recent bank statement, recent retirement statement, medical insurance card copy, tax returns, home and car insurance documents, photos of inside and outside of house (in case needed for insurance), information on trusts and bonds.

Identity: Birth certificates, copies of passports, degree certificates, social security card copies.

Will: Copy of recent wills and end of life directives.

Miscellaneous: Other useful documents such as lists of phone numbers and address books.

Software: Any software installation packages you would need to recover files, such as a password manager like KeePassXC and VeraCrypt.

I also recommend creating a "Read Me" document as a narrative that describes everything in the folder.

This will also be useful in the case of your death for family members working through your stuff.

Once you have created an electronic copy, you should then create a paper copy and keep it in a secure place such as a safe. I also recommend keeping a copy on an encrypted USB flash drive on your keyring with the critical family documents archive on it.

Robust Digital Backup System Checklist

- ☐ Decide on the backup strategy that is right for you
- ☐ Set up desired synchronization services
- ☐ Buy offline backup storage device (SSD or USB stick)
- ☐ Encrypt offline backup storage device with VeraCrypt
- ☐ Complete first offline backup
- ☐ Implement photos and videos backup strategy
- ☐ Install Thunderbird and add all email accounts you want to back up
- ☐ Download social media archives and store in backed up folder
- ☐ Create electronic and paper critical family documents archive

Chapter Three
Digitally Resilient Internet Use

The Internet is where almost everything happens in our digital lives, good or bad. In this chapter I will describe how to maximize the reliability and availability of your Internet connection, using it in a way that increases security and privacy, and you'll learn about ways to make everything work better, such as using a password manager, email forwarding and a credit card masking service.

Reliable and redundant Internet access

For most people, the majority of Internet access is either with a home Internet service through a company such as AT&T or Comcast, or with a mobile Internet service on a smartphone. I will cover the home Internet connection in this chapter, and will discuss mobile Internet in the chapter on smartphones. The first step in digital resilient Internet use is to maximize the reliability of your Internet connection, and to provide some redundancy if possible. In many areas there is unfortunately little or no choice in Internet Service Providers (ISPs), but if you do have a choice it is worth doing research on the reliability and speed of the available Internet services. Much of this is hyper-local, dependent on the quality and state of cabling in your neighborhood, so asking neighbors is a great place to start. You can get an idea of the overall reliability of services on the Outage Report website (**https://outage.report**), which shows historically reported outages by date and geographic location. For example, the outage history of Xfinity, Comcast's product, is at **https://outage.report/us/xfinity**. If you already have a home Internet service, test the speed of your connection using the Speed Test website (**https://www.speedtest.net**). The most accurate results will be gained by having a physical Ethernet connection between your testing computer and your router, but if this is not possible, go as close to your router as you can. Your speed is theoretically related to the level of service you pay for, with more expensive plans advertising higher speeds, although there is a lot of variation in the actual speed that people receive. Generally, if you are seeing speeds above 20mbps (megabits per second), you will likely be able to carry out most Internet activities at reasonable speed. If you are a gamer, or have several people streaming video at once, you will want to be closer to 60mbps as a minimum. If you think there is a speed or reliability problem with your Internet connection, don't hesitate to contact the ISP and ask for a service visit to test the connection to the outside of your house. Ask in advance whether this will incur a service fee: even if it does, in the long run it will be worth it. For an in-depth comparison of ISPs as well as guides on what service you need, check out the USA Today site at **https://www.usnews.com/360-reviews/internet-providers/best-internet-providers**.

The Internet speed and reliability will also be affected by the hardware that you are using. There are two important pieces of hardware related to the Internet: the *cable modem* which enables computer network communication over cable or fiber lines, and the *router*, usually a wireless router, which provides network and Internet access to your computers and devices. The cable modem will be connected to your ISP's cable line, and the router will be connected to the cable modem via an *ethernet cable*. In some cases, the router and cable modem might be in the same box. Often, an ISP will provide their own cable modem or combined cable modem and router and charge you a monthly fee for it, but most allow you to also purchase your own cable modem and all allow you to use your own router. I recommend that you purchase your own cable modem and router, and have them as separate devices. This increases the control that you have over your technology, and in the long run it will likely save you money. Most cable modems cost around $100, and routers $100-300. If you have an old modem or router, then upgrading is a good idea, as more recent models are more efficient, more secure and better performing. For routers, make sure it is compatible with the recent wireless networking standard 802.11ac, often designated by an "AC" in the model name or description. The number following AC designates the theoretical maximum bandwidth in megabits per second (mbps), so for example an AC1900 router is faster than an AC1750. I recommend at least AC1750. My preferred routers are the Netgear Nighthawk series (**https://www.netgear.com/landings/nighthawk**).

Given how critical the Internet is to our daily lives, I recommend that you always have two methods available to access the Internet. If you have a smartphone, your cellular service can be your second method. This is made even more useful if your phone can be used as a hotspot (effectively a wireless router) so other devices can use the Internet on your phone. If you can afford it, an ideal solution for Internet backup is to have a dedicated *mobile hotspot* with data service. Most cellular providers offer a data-only plan for hotspots. Choose a hotspot device such as the Nighthawk (**https://www.netgear.com/landings/nighthawk-mr1100-mobile-router**) that has a built-in Ethernet port. This means that if your regular Internet service goes down, you can simply remove the Ethernet cable from the Cable Modem and plug it into the hotspot.

Secure your WiFi

Router security is an important piece of your digital resilience strategy. There are a few steps you should take to ensure your router is secure. First, you will need to figure out how to access your router administration page. This is done using a numeric IP address on your local network. The IP address is usually on a label on the bottom of the router along with default username and password. It is almost always one of 192.168.1.1, 192.168.0.1 or 10.0.0.1. Go to a browser, and type this number is as if it were a web address. You should then see the login page for the router administration page. Type in the username and password (either the one on the router, or one you have set).

First make sure you have a secure password for the administration panel. The default is usually a username of "admin" and a password of "password". If you leave it like this, it means anyone in range of your router can hack into your network. In the administration page, find where you can change the password and instead change it to a strong password (preferably created by a password manager – see below). Also look for an option for "remote access" to the administration panel. If this is enabled, it means your router administration page can be accessed from anywhere on the Internet. This is a bad thing, so ensure that it is disabled. Finally, go to the wireless settings, and make sure that the wireless security protocol is set to WPA or WPA2, not WEP, to ensure good encryption on your wireless traffic, and while you are at it make sure you have a secure password for access to the wireless network.

Lock down your browser

Your Internet browser is the gateway to the Global Cloud. It is very important that you take some steps to make your browser more resilient and secure.

There are several browsers available, the most widely used being Chrome, Microsoft Edge, Microsoft Internet Explorer, Firefox and Safari. The two browsers I recommend are Firefox (**https://www.mozilla.org/en-US/firefox**) and Brave (**https://brave.com**). These two browsers are designed with privacy and security in mind, have the least amount of data collection and analytics, and are the easiest to set up in a resilient way. If you are using one of the other browsers, consider making the switch – it's really quite easy, especially since you can export bookmarks from your existing browser and import them into the new one. I recommend installing both browsers on your machine, which gives you some redundancy, and can be useful if a particular website doesn't work properly on one browser.

Once Firefox or Brave is installed, there are some important settings to change to maintain security and privacy. In particular these will ensure that you are using a relatively private search engine, and that the websites you visit can't learn as much about the other websites you visit.

For Firefox, click on the ≡ (menu) icon and select "Preferences". Under "General" make Firefox your default browser, and turn off "Recommend extensions as you browse" and "Recommend features as you browse". Under "Home", select which content you want to see on the opening page. Under "Search", I recommend making the default search engine DuckDuckGo (better privacy than Google) and turn off search suggestions. Under "Privacy & Security" click "Delete cookies and site data when Firefox is closed", and turn off "Ask to save logins and passwords for websites" (you will use a separate password manager for this). In the "History" section, select "Firefox will Use custom settings for history", turn of "Remember browsing and download history" and "Remember search and form history", and check "Clear history when Firefox closes". At the side, click Settings, and make sure all boxes are checked including "Site Preferences" and "Offline Website Data". Turn off all Firefox Data Collection and Use options.

Now add three extensions that will reduce the amount of data collection when you visit websites. The first is a tool that blocks trackers that websites try to install on your browser. Click on "Extensions & Themes" in the left panel, then search for and install "uBlock Origin". Once it is installed, try going to a popular news site like CNN.com. The small shield icon in the top corner will let you know how many trackers have been blocked on the page. This will reduce the ability of sites to track your behavior.

The second extension is called *HTTPS Everywhere*. It will ensure that every time you go to a website it uses HTTPS rather than HTTP, which means the traffic between your computer and the website will be encrypted. Again, you can search for this under "Extensions & Themes" in the settings.

The third extension will enable you to compartmentalize different tabs and pages so they can't interact with each other. Search for "Firefox Multi-Account Containers", and install. Once it is installed it will lead you through how to set it up, so that you can compartmentalize different tabs for different functions – for example social media, shopping, work and personal.

For Brave, set things up a little differently. Click on the ≡ (menu) icon and select Settings. All the settings are shown in one long page, so I will walk through this in order from top to bottom. Under Get started, select "Open the New Tab Page" for what to open when the browser starts. Under "New Tab Page", you can set what appears on a new tab page: I recommend turning everything off, although if you want to leave on some decoration such as the background image or the clock, that is fine. Under "Shields", Brave has some nice options for blocking ads and upgrading to HTTPS. I recommend keeping "Trackers and ads blocking" as Standard, ensure "Upgrade connection to HTTPS" is on, and leave "Cookie blocking and Fingerprinting blocking" as "Only cross-site" and Standard respectively. Under social media blocking, I usually keep these off, but this will mean that you won't see embedded Tweets, LinkedIn and Facebook posts in web pages. Under search engine, select DuckDuckGo. Now click on **Additional Settings > Privacy and Security** in the panel at the left. Turn all of the buttons off in this section. Under "WebRTC IP Handling Policy", select Default public interface only (this will stop any leak of your local network connection information when using video). Click on "Clear browsing data", select the "On exit" tab, and make sure everything is selected. Since Brave does its own tracker blocking and HTTPS enforcement, you don't strictly need to add in the uBlock Origin or HTTPS Everywhere extensions, but I like to anyway as a second line of defense. You can install them through the Extensions option in the panel on the left.

Password and security management

The weakest link in the digital resilience of most people is their Internet password and security strategy. The need to have usernames and passwords for tens or maybe even hundreds of accounts is a nightmare to manage, and so our natural tendency is to reuse the same usernames and passwords across different sites, and to use simple passwords. This means that if our password is stolen from one site, attackers can likely get access to our accounts on other sites. Through a series of online breaches and security failings of popular sites over the last few years, many passwords and email-password combinations are already in hacker databases available on the Internet. It is well worth going to **https://haveibeenpwned.com** and checking your email and passwords to see if they have already been breached. Even if not, it is time now to move to a much more secure way of managing your Internet accounts.

Fortunately, there is an easy way to deal with this problem: using a password manager. A password manager is a program that both generates secure passwords, and stores those passwords along with other account information in a secure way. It is the digital equivalent of a password book. Some password managers store your passwords in the Cloud, but this is a little beyond my comfort zone. If you have implemented the backup strategy in Chapter 2, there is no reason you need your passwords to be stored anywhere but your own devices and your secure backups. If you do really want to have a cloud-based password manager, I would recommend BitWarden (**https://bitwarden.com/**). My preferred password manager is KeePassXC (**https://keepassxc.org/**), an open-source password manager that stores your passwords in one or more encrypted files on your local machine. So long as these files are stored in your synchronization / backed-up folder, and you implement your full backup strategy, you are at low risk of losing your passwords, and also low risk of having them breached. Here

I will walk through using KeePassXC to generate and store your passwords.

KeePassXC is available for MacOS, Windows and Linux. Third party apps are available for smartphones that can read and write KeePassXC files – these will be covered in the smartphone chapter. Download and install the correct client for your operating system. Depending on your needs, you may decide to have more than one password file – for example, one for work and one for personal – or keep everything in the same file. To create a new KeePassXC password file, open the application and choose **Database > New Database**. You will be asked for a database name and optional description. On the next screen you have the option to change the encryption settings. I think the settings are fine, so click "Continue". You will then need to create a master password for your passwords file. If you are lucky, this could be the only password you ever have to remember again except for your computer password. Make sure it is very secure as described in Chapter 1. You can then click Done. Now choose a location to save the passwords file – this should be somewhere in the folder that will be backed up and/or synchronized. Congratulations! You now have a new password file. Now you need to populate it.

Below I describe a process to create an entry in the password file for each of your online accounts. I recommend starting with a few of the most important accounts to you – maybe email, social media and your bank. Create an entry and test it using your existing password and credentials for each account. Once you are comfortable with using KeePassXC, you can beef up the security by getting the password manager to select new, very secure passwords for your accounts. At that time you can also add *two factor authentication* for services that provide it.

KeePassXC lets you organize your account details into folders, much like file folders. By default, everything is in a single folder called "Root". I prefer to rename this to something more meaningful, like "Personal Accounts". To do this, right click (control click on MacOS) on the Root folder and choose "Edit Group…" to edit the name of the folder. You can create new folders by clicking on the folder icon in the toolbar, and folders and accounts can be dragged around the panel to the left. You can now create a new account entry – let's say you have a ProtonMail.com account with the username myname@protonmail.com and password "blueBear2000". Click on the plus-in-a-circle icon on the toolbar, and a window will open up with boxes to add entries for Title, Username, Password, URL (of the service), an optional expiration date and time, and notes. I prefer to just use the name of the service for the title, but you can use this as you wish. The password will by default be masked as you type, but if you click on the eye icon beside it, the password will be shown. When filled out, this should look something like Figure 3.1. The other tabs in the panel allow you to some things like changing the icon and adding attachments. When you are done entering your first account, click OK and move onto the next. The password file will be auto-saved every time you create a new entry. When you are done, you should see a list of accounts in the main panel of KeePassXC.

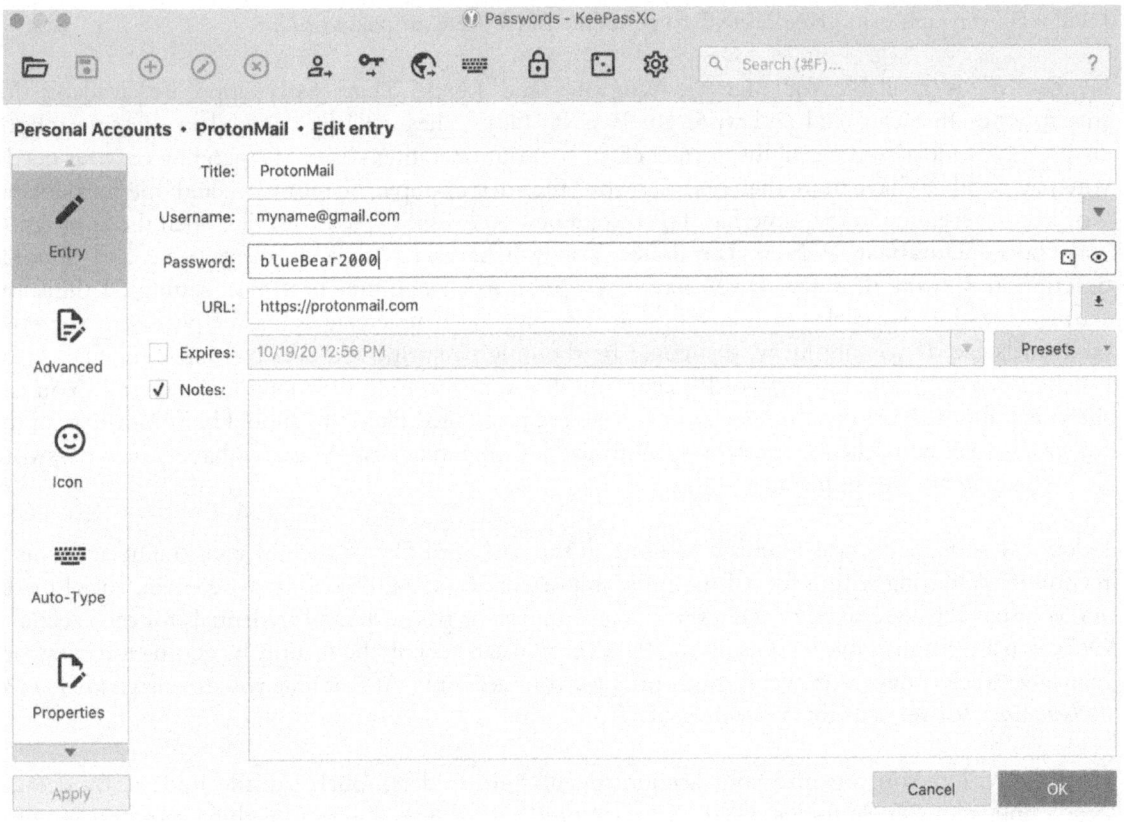

Figure 3.1. Example account entry in KeePassXC.

Now try using KeePassXC to log onto one of your accounts. I will stick with the ProtonMail example. Open up KeePassXC, and double-click on the URL of the account that you want to sign into, in this case ProtonMail. ProtonMail will then open in your browser, with boxes to type your username and password. Keep the Facebook entry selected in KeePassXC and click on the "copy username" icon (the sixth icon from the left, the one that looks like a person with an arrow). The username is then in the clipboard, and you can go back to the ProtonMail page and paste it into the box (Control V, or ⌘ V on MacOS). You will now be asked for your password. In KeePassXC, click on the key icon to the right of the username icon to copy your password to the clipboard. Now go back to the browser and press Control or ⌘ V in the password box to paste in your password. You can now happily forget your password, as you no longer need to even know what it is!

If all of this seems a bit too much work, then there is an easier way. KeePassXC has a browser plug-in for most browsers called KeePassXC-Browser, that will automatically fill out usernames and passwords for you so you don't have to do all that cutting and pasting. First you will need to enable browser integration in KeePassXC (**Preferences > Browser Integration > Enable browser integration**). On this page you can select which browser you want to use, and links are provided to install the plug-in for your browser. Once installed in your browser, you will see a small KeePassXC icon in your browser toolbar. Click this, then click the button to configure the link with your KeePassXC application on the desktop. You will need to provide a name for the link, and then you are ready to go. Sticking with the ProtonMail example, if you now go to the Facebook website, you should see a box popping up from KeePassXC asking if it's OK to share information about your ProtonMail account with the plug-in (and if you have multiple accounts, you can select which ones to share). Click Allow Selected. You should now see a green KeePassXC icon in the login box on ProtonMail. If you click this, your credentials will be automatically inserted. If you have more than one account, you will be allowed to select which one you want to use. The KeePassXC browser plug-in isn't perfect – for example with sites like Google where username and password are entered on separate screens, it often doesn't work properly. However, it does make things very convenient. My own preference is to stick with cut-and-pasting from the KeePassXC application, but you can make your own decision on this.

Once you have entered your accounts into KeePassXC, have become comfortable using it to log into your accounts and have made sure to back up your password file, you can start the process of improving the security of your accounts. For each account, you will ask KeePassXC to generate a new, very secure password for the account, as well as enabling two-factor authentication where available. I will use the ProtonMail example above. First, log onto your account, and find the correct place on the site to change your password. Enter in your existing password to the "current password" or equivalent box. Now go to KeePassXC, double click to open up the account, and click on the small square box beside the password entry. This will open up a window that will let you generate a new password (see Figure 3.2). Make sure that the length is set to at least 20 characters. You can also select the character types that are included in the password – capital letters, lower case letters, numbers, and symbols. In the box at the top of the window you can see the random password that has automatically been generated for you. In this case the new password is "0pQypc8evcJ7XfdiVMSO". This is of course unlike "blueBear2000" impossible to remember, but now you don't need to remember it, as the password manager does the work for you, and you will have a very secure, unique password for each account. Click "Apply Password", and this new password will now be inserted into the password box overwriting your old password. Click "OK" to save the entry. Now click on the password icon to copy the new password into the clipboard, and paste it into the "New Password" entry on the website. Finish up the new password process on the website, then try logging in again to make sure the new password works.

Whenever you create a new Internet account, be sure to use the password generator to create a secure password for the account. The "notes" section is also a great place to store additional information about your account in a secure way.

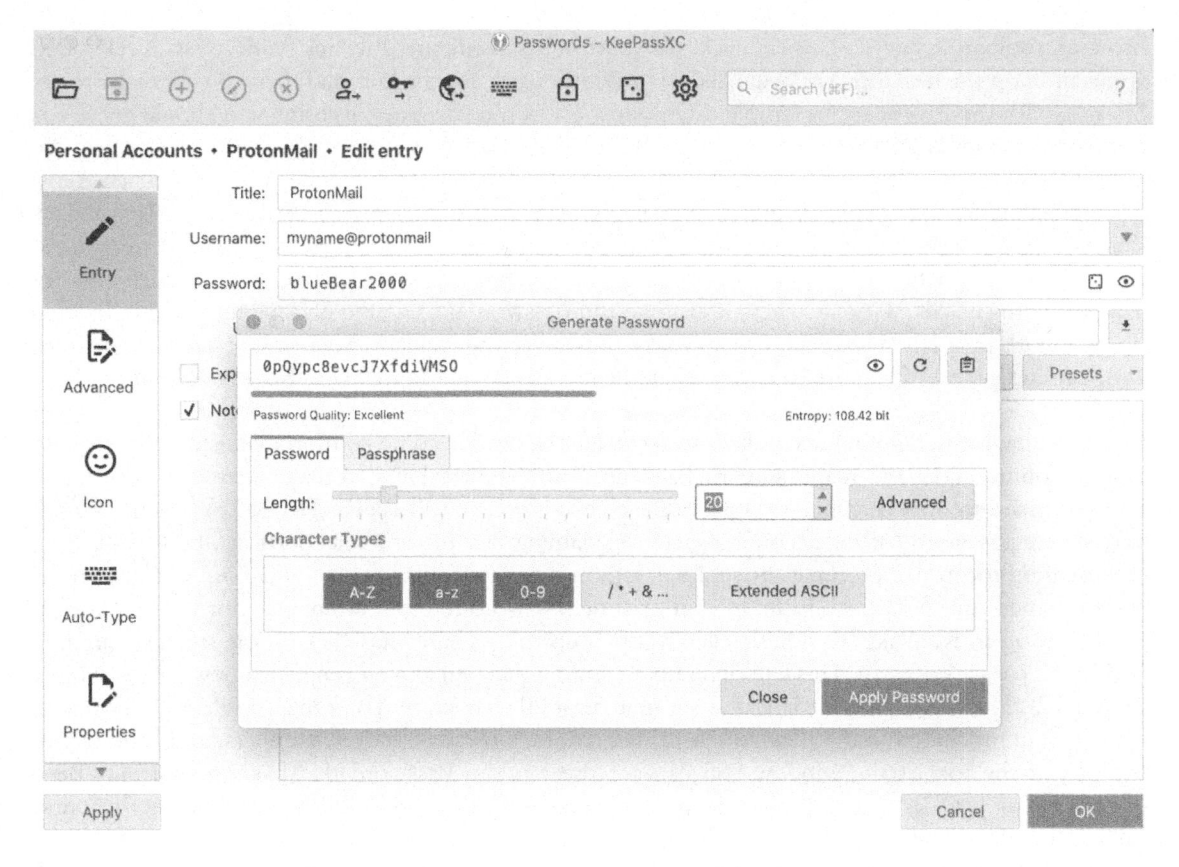

Figure 3.2. Generating a new password for an account.

Two-Factor Authentication (TFA), sometimes called Multi-Factor Authentication (MFA) is a way to increase the security of your online accounts by requiring an additional authentication step when you log in, usually the entry of a one-time PIN number (OTP). Some websites will do this automatically by requiring you to type in a PIN number that is sent to your email or phone account – banks are particularly fond of this method. This vastly increases your security, but if your email or phone account is compromised the security is lost. More secure is to use an *authenticator application* on your smartphone. Commonly used authenticators are Google Authenticator, Duo and Twilio Authy. Options to enable TFA can usually be found in the settings of the website or app where you have an account. The process usually involves the site showing you a QR code (2D barcode) which you scan with the camera of your smartphone in the authenticator app. I strongly recommend that you right-click (control-click on MacOS) on the image of the QR code and save it to a secure location, so that if you change or lose your smartphone you can activate the authentication on another device. You can also attach this image to the entry in KeePassXC if you are comfortable having your password and authenticator information in the same place. The app will then have a rolling 6-digit number which changes every minute. When you next log onto the website, you will be asked to enter the six-digit number that is showing in the authenticator app for that website. Using TFA vastly improves your account security, as it means that it is almost impossible for someone to access your account without access to your smartphone as well as your username and password.

Protect your IP address with a VPN

Internet Protocol addresses, or *IP addresses* for short, are unique identifiers that are assigned to devices that are attached to the Internet. An IP address might look something like 208.80.154.232. When you activate a cable modem with an ISP, the modem – and by extension everything connected to it – will use this IP address to identify itself on the Internet. Similarly, smartphones will be assigned an IP address by the cellular provider. Sometimes IP addresses change frequently, but sometimes you can keep the same IP address for years. Most IP addresses are in the *IPv4* format which is four sets of numbers separated by dots. Recently, the IPv6 standard came in with a longer, more complex format. All websites that you visit get access to your IP address, which can be used to uniquely identify your network or device as well as your approximate geographic location. You can see your current IP address along with the estimated location by going to **https://whatismyipaddress.com**. Note that this IP address is different than the local area network address, which uses the same protocol, but just identifies devices on your local area network, usually those attached to your router. These will usually have the format 192.168.x.x or 10.0.x.x.

You can use a Virtual Private Network service, or VPN, to prevent websites from being able to see your true IP address. When you are using a VPN, instead of connecting directly to a website, your computer makes an encrypted "secure tunnel" through to a special VPN server located elsewhere. This server then makes the connection to the destination website, and it is the IP address of the server that the website sees. So for example, you might live in New York, but connect to a VPN server in Stockholm. Your IP address would appear to websites as if you were connecting from Stockholm. VPNs serve three basic purposes: they mask your true IP address from websites; they hide your website activity from your ISP; and they help make using public WiFi more secure as the secure tunnel reduces the risk that someone could intercept your web traffic. VPNs do not really make your web surfing truly anonymous. State actors can quite easily map the incoming traffic to the VPN server to the outgoing traffic to the website. But they do give you a level of protection in your Internet usage, and they stop websites from being able to easily identify your location and to track activity from your IP address.

It is important to choose a VPN that you trust, as the VPN service gets to see all of your web browsing information. There are many shady free VPN services out there. An exhaustive comparison of VPN providers can be found at **https://thatoneprivacysite.net**. The two VPN services that I recommend are ProtonVPN (**https://protonvpn.com**) and Mullvad (**https://mullvad.net**). Both of these services have ethics and business models strongly committed to privacy, have a range of servers throughout the world, and do not keep usage logs. ProtonVPN offers a basic free service with servers in the USA and New Zealand, but it is well worth upgrading to the ProtonVPN Basic ($4 or €4/month) or Plus ($8 or €8/month) for faster speeds and the ability to have multiple connections at once. Mullvad offers monthly service for €5/month.

The easiest way to start using the VPN is to download the app for your computer or device. This will then make a direct connection between your computer and the VPN server. Some routers allow you to enable a VPN service within the router, especially if you have installed the open source DD-WRT software (**https://dd-wrt.com**) on your router. This is advantageous in that any device that is connected to the router will then automatically be connected to the VPN without having to activate software on the device, and without risk of losing protection if the VPN app crashes or fails. The disadvantage is that because routers generally have slower processors than computers and devices, Internet access speeds will be much slower on a router running a VPN – typically around 10-20mbps.

One good option can be to install DD-WRT on an old router, set it up with a different WiFi name to your main network, activate your VPN on this router, then plug it into your main router with an Ethernet cable. You will then have a separate WiFi that you can join that is VPN protected, albeit at slower speeds. Instructions for installing ProtonVPN on a router can be found at **https://protonvpn.com/support/installing-protonvpn-on-a-router** and for Mullvad at **https://mullvad.net/en/help/dd-wrt-routers-and-mullvad-vpn**).

If you really want to activate a whole-house VPN without a speed cost, the way to do it is with a computer or dedicated firewall running PFSense (**https://www.pfsense.org**) – but that does require some fairly advanced computing skills to set up.

Evaluating online services for resilience

Most of us incorporate many online services in our daily lives, and don't think too much about how much we depend on them until there is a problem with the service – maybe an outage, or our account gets locked, or there is a big data breach in the news. How resilient an online service needs to be will depend on how critical it is for your life, what could go wrong if it goes away, and what personal data you are entrusting the service with. How can you ensure that the online services that are critical for your lives are digitally resilient? Here is a four-step plan:

1. Ensure you have a reliable Internet service with at least one backup
2. Critically evaluate your online services for resilience
3. Have and regularly use an alternate for any critical services
4. Have a non-Internet backup plan for anything that is critical

The first, I have already covered. Critical evaluation of online services should focus on the following:

- *Terms of service.* How committed is the company to the privacy and security of your data? What will they do with your data? Can they give or sell it to third parties? What happens if they decide to close your account?
- *Business model.* What is the ongoing cost of using the service? If it is a free service, you might have less confidence in it than a paid service. What is the business model? What is the risk of the company closing the service or going bankrupt? Do you trust the company? Do other people trust the company? If open source, is it well supported?
- *Data security.* Is your data encrypted when it is stored on the company's servers? Is it zero knowledge end-to-end encryption? Does the service offer two-factor authentication?
- *Reliability.* What is the uptime of the service? What historical outages have there been (check **https://downdetector.com** for outage history of commonly used services)? What

infrastructure does it depend on (e.g. Amazon Web Services)? Can you still use the service and access your data offline?
- *Extractability.* Can you download your data in a format that would make it easy to back up and restore, or to switch to another service?

For each critical service, you should find an alternate that runs as much as possible on a different infrastructure. For example, if videoconferencing is a critical service for you, then you might use Zoom as your primary service, and Microsoft Teams as your backup. Zoom runs on Amazon Web Services, and Teams on the Azure Cloud, so if one of the cloud systems goes down the chances are the other will still work. You should regularly alternate between the two to make sure you are familiar with their use and your account is kept current.

Email strategy

If you are like most people, you probably use the same email address for everything. You probably also get large amounts of junk email, and are on plenty of lists that you would rather get off. Using the same email across sites is also a security and privacy risk, because it enables using your email as a common identifier to link different accounts together. Here I present a strategy for using email that will allow you to compartmentalize, that will prevent your "real" email addresses from being seen by every website on which you create an account, and that will help you get better control of your email.

The first question is whether it is time for an email "fresh start". Creating a new email account is very easy, and gives you the opportunity to be careful to decide with whom you want to share the new email address. It also allows you to select a different email provider if you wish. If you go this route, it is relatively simple to set up your old email account to forward all emails to your new one – for example on Gmail you can do this by going to **Settings > Forwarding and POP/IMAP > Add a forwarding address**. On your new account, you can set up a filter to automatically put email from the old account into a separate folder (e.g. "Legacy email") which you can check occasionally without having your new inbox clogged up. Now that you hopefully have a clean, fresh email account, I would recommend only giving this email address out to real people with whom you want to engage in conversation. For all the other purposes, create email forwarding accounts that will let you create custom email addresses for different sites.

I am going to describe two ways of using email forwarding, using your own domain name, and using a forwarding service such as Anonaddy (**https://anonaddy.com**). My recommendation is that you use your own domain name for accounts that are important to you and where you want to make sure you don't lose control of the email address – your bank, utilities, and so on – and then use a forwarding service for "junk" accounts that you need to create maybe for one-offs or where you are not sure what your data will be used for. Setting up your own domain is a little bit of work and expense, but I think it is well worth it in the long run. However, you may decide to just use the email forwarding and use your existing email address for important accounts.

Let's start with setting up your own domain. A domain name is the name that is given to an internet domain like "google.com" or "wikipedia.org". You can buy domain names for a relatively cheap annual fee from companies such as GoDaddy (**https://godaddy.com**) or Namecheap (**https://namecheap.com**) and set them up for handling both email and websites. Since the opening up of new top-level domains a few years ago, there are many options for domain names. I suggest selecting a domain name that doesn't directly identify you, but that looks like something valid. You can start by typing something of interest to you in GoDaddy's or Namecheap's search box and see what comes up. For example, if you love Airedale Terrier dogs, you could search for something like "airedale". This will likely come up with some expensive options ("Airedale.net" is available for $3,999) and plenty of cheap ones. I suggest you choose something with a .com, .org or .net ending, as these look more familiar and established, but anything is okay. At the time of writing, "airdaleworld.com" is available for $11.99/year at GoDaddy, so let's say you choose that. When you go through the process of registering be careful about the decisions you make: for example, for an extra fee you can add privacy to your domain registration so that your personal details are not made public. I strongly recommend doing this. Your domain will likely come with "email forwarding" but if you have the option make sure to select this.

Once your domain is paid for and set up, you can then set it up to forward emails. If you are using the domain just for email forwarding, I think GoDaddy is the easiest to set up. I will show you how to set up a "catch all" that will forward all emails to your new domain to your existing email address. On GoDaddy, go to **Workspace Email > Manage All**. click on "Create Forward" in the table, and you will see a window as shown in Figure 3.3. In the Forward this email address box, type "anything@*yourdomain*"; for example "anything@airdaleworld.com". In the next box, enter your real email address. Select "Make this a catch-all account", then click Create. It will take GoDaddy just a few minutes to set up the forward. You now will have any email sent to your domain forwarded to your real email address: I will describe shortly how this is fantastically useful for your Internet accounts. First, make sure it is working. Send an email to test@*yourdomain* – for example test@airdaleworld.com – and make sure you receive the email that has been forwarded.

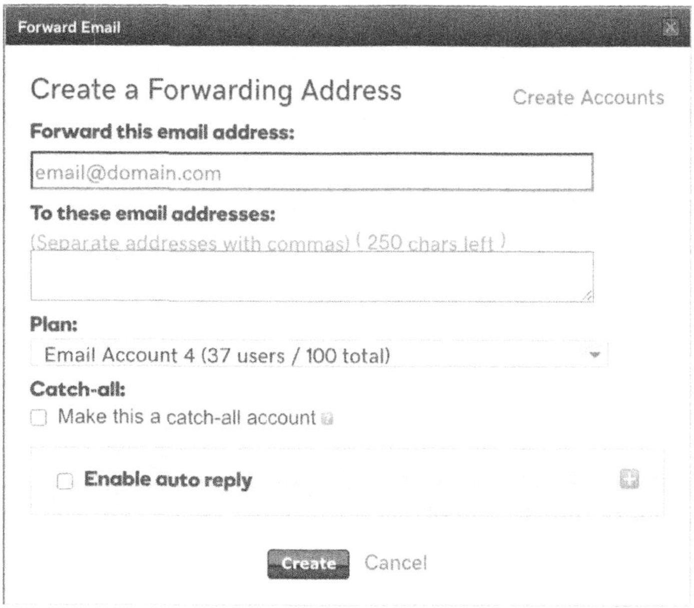

Figure 3.3. Email forwarding window in GoDaddy.

You now have the capability to create completely custom email addresses for any purpose. I recommend using the name of the service you are using as the "name" part of the email. For example, if you have an Amazon.com account and your domain is airdaleworld.com, you can use the email amazon@airdaleworld.com. For Facebook, you can use facebook@airdaleworld.com. Note that you can add additional forwarding entries that will override the "catch all", so if you want to compartmentalize where your email is forwarded to, you can do that too. For example, let's say your name is Bob, email bob@gmail.com and your significant other is called Alice, email alice@gmail.com. You can create a forwarding entry to forward facebookbob@airdaleworld.com to bob@gmail.com and facebookalice@airdaleworld.com to alice@gmail.com. This way, Internet services will never get to see your "real" email address, and if your credentials are compromised on one site, the email will not be valid on any other site. This should also stop companies tracking you across sites by your email address. You can also set up custom filters to move email for a particular account into a special folder, or even delete them if you want to. I have a filter set up so that any email that has my forwarding domain in the "To" field will get sent to a special accounts folder. As you update your existing accounts with your new email forwarding addresses, be sure to update your password manager accordingly.

A similar effect can be had by using a third-party email forwarding service, such as AnonAddy. For free, you can set up a subdomain of AnonAddy to use as a forwarding email. For example, you could select "airdaleworld.anonaddy.com" and then a message sent to *anything*@airdaleworld.anonaddy.com will be forwarded to your real address. The advantage is that you do not have to purchase and set up your own domain name, and AnonAddy gives you the option to block any email names you no longer which to receive email from. The disadvantage is that you don't own the domain name, and AnonAddy could withdraw it at any time, meaning you lose access to the email that goes to the domain. Further,

AnonAddy does get to see all the email that gets forwarded to you. Also some sites will not accept email addresses from these forwarding services. For this reason, I recommend using third-party forwarding services only for "junk" purposes – for example when a website insists you give an email address to download something, or for newsletters and so on. You can even forward to your domain: for example, @airdaleworld.anonaddy.com could forward to anonaddy@airdaileworld.com, which would then be forwarded to your "real" email.

Avoiding phishing and ransomware attacks

Phishing is a malicious attempt to obtain sensitive information or data from you such as identity details, account information, or credit card numbers, by sending an email or text message to you that looks like a real message from a site that you might expect to receive, but instead tricks you into providing your details in a return email, entering them on a malicious spoofed site, or installing malicious code on your computer or device. Most phishing email attempts are very general, usually saying there is a problem with an account, and that you need to click to put something right. An example is given in Figure 3.4, and you can see further examples at **https://www.phishing.org/phishing-examples**.

Figure 3.4. Example PayPal phishing attempt, taken from https://www.phishing.org/phishing-examples

Spearphishing is a special kind of Phishing attack that is specially customized for you, that targets you individually. So let's say your name is Joe, your boss at work is called Sarah, and you work on a big project called Archimedes. In a spearphishing attack, someone will have researched you personally, so you might receive an email that says something like: "Joe – Sarah here. Sending this from my personal account, a big problem has come up with Archimedes project, customer needs updated info now. Can you log on here and answer the customer's question? [malicious link]".

Similar techniques are used to introduce *Ransomware*, a destructive kind of malware that encrypts everything on your drive, and possibly your network, with malicious actors demanding a ransom to unencrypt your files, usually to be paid in Bitcoin.

You can vastly reduce your risk of being a victim of a phishing or ransomware attack with just two simple steps.

1. Never click on any link in an unsolicited email or text message. By unsolicited, I mean an email that you are not immediately expecting. So, for example, when you sign up for a new online account, the site will likely send you a verification email with a link to click. This would be a *solicited* email. If you get an email that appears to be from one of your accounts, like the PayPal example above, do not click on a link in the email. Instead, go to the site, such as **https://paypal.com**, log in, and check there to see if there really is an issue to be dealt with.

2. Keep your browser up to date. Browsers such as Firefox have built-in checks to look for common malicious sites and warn you about them. You can read more about how Firefox does this at **https://support.mozilla.org/en-US/kb/how-does-phishing-and-malware-protection-work**.

Masked credit cards

Using your credit card to sign up for goods and services online is risky. Many sites have poor security, and become victims of hackers who steal account information including stored credit card details. Plus any time you give your credit card details to a third party, you are trusting them to only bill you for what you are expecting to be billed for. Many of us have had the problem of seeing recurring billings on our credit card bill for a service we thought we had canceled.

Masked credit card services like Privacy (**https://privacy.com**) and Abine Blur (**https://www.abine.com**) allow you to use "disposable" credit cards that are linked to your bank account. You can set up a custom credit card number for one-off use, or tied to a particular merchant, with limits set on the amount that can be billed to the card. When a charge is made, it is debited directly from your bank account. At any time you can pause or delete a credit card to ensure that no more transactions can be made on it. My personal favorite is Privacy.com which has iOS and Android apps to using masked credit cards easy.

An added benefit of masked credit cards is that you can use any name, address and ZIP code with them. So you don't have to give your real details to a website just to make a purchase.

Planting your flag

In general, I am in favor of only creating online accounts that you actually need. But there are some online accounts and services that are worth securing now, in order to prevent someone else pretending to be you from getting access to them. For example, many states in the U.S. have online systems for claiming unemployment benefits that require you to create an account. Incredibly, often all you need to create an account is your name, your date of birth, and your city of residence, all information that is likely easily accessible to hackers. If you create an account now with a secure password, you will prevent someone else from creating it in your name.

For more on this, read Brian Krebs' blog post at **https://krebsonsecurity.com/2020/08/why-where-you-should-you-plant-your-flag**.

Smart devices in your home

A chapter on Internet usage wouldn't be complete without addressing the proliferation of "smart home" devices that are now available. Smart home devices are meant to provide function or service in your home, and are usually Internet connected. Devices include smart speakers such as Alexa and Google Home, cameras, thermostats, smart refrigerators, light bulbs, and so on. My overall recommendation is to be very careful about introducing smart devices into your home, particularly for critical functions like controlling your heating and air conditioning. Do you really need to be able to control your thermostat from the other side of the world? If you do see a need for smart devices, look for ones that can work on a local network without connecting to the Internet. If you do need devices connected to the Internet, all the usual rules apply: make sure the accounts are secured with a strong password and two-factor authentication, and avoid using email addresses or other identifying information where possible.

Digitally Resilient Internet Use Checklist

- ☐ Review your home Internet service and see if improvements to reliability or speed need to be made, either by contacting your ISP or switching to an alternative
- ☐ Identify a backup for Internet in case your primary service goes out (e.g. smartphone hotspot)
- ☐ Update your router and cable modem if necessary
- ☐ Secure your WiFi router
- ☐ Select Firefox or Brave as a primary browser, and lock it down using the instructions provided
- ☐ Install KeePassXC or another password manager. Migrate your accounts to use strong passwords generated by the password manager
- ☐ Enable two-factor authentication on all important accounts, where available
- ☐ Create a fresh personal email account; forward your existing email with a filter to move it to a legacy email folder
- ☐ Set up an email forwarding system using your own domain name and/or a forwarding service such as Anonaddy
- ☐ Review steps for securing against phishing and ransomware attacks
- ☐ Set up a masked credit card system with Privacy.com or Blur as desired
- ☐ Set up a credit freeze, and proactively create any accounts you think needed to "plant your flag"
- ☐ Review your usage of smart home devices

Chapter Four

A Digitally Resilient Smartphone

Smartphones are incredible inventions. We have a world of information on the Internet at our fingertips wherever we go, can communicate with family and friends reliably, and have access to countless apps to entertain us and to support our work and life. But smartphones are also problematic. Our reliance on them means if we lose connectivity our lives can become difficult. They are effectively tracking devices, meaning that we are constantly revealing our location to who knows how many companies. They are windows to the Internet, so all the security and privacy risks we have with the Internet come with smartphones. The good news is that with some carefully thought out changes, you can mitigate many of these problems. In this chapter, you will learn how to use a smartphone in a way that is robust, secure, private and under your control. The steps in this chapter can also be mostly applied to tablets such as iPads.

Selecting a phone

There are really only two kinds of smartphone in common use: iOS devices from Apple, and Android devices from other manufacturers that use Google services along with the open source Android operating system. In the chapter on advanced digital resilience, I describe a third option – a de-Googled version of Android – but for now I will consider just these two options. This does mean that if you use a smartphone you are tied into an Apple or Google ecosystem.

Overall, I believe iOS devices are better than Google-enabled Androids for digital resilience. Apple makes highly reliable and robust devices, with excellent privacy and security. Although some information is shared with Apple, the company's business model seems to be more focused on product sales than Google's model of monetizing your data. iOS devices are easy to back up and restore onto a new device, at least if you have an Apple computer. Make sure you are using a version of the iPhone that is compatible with the latest iOS 14, as this has the best privacy and security features. This means at least an original iPhone SE or 6S. I recommend at least an iPhone 8 to ensure that updates will continue for a good period. The new iPhone SE is an excellent budget-level phone.

If you do decide to use an Android, be sure that the phone you buy uses Android 11, the most recent version of the operating system, as it has some big improvements in privacy and security. My recommendation is that you consider one of the Google Pixel phones (**https://pixel.google.com**), as they are robust, get frequent operating system updates, and have hardware which makes it easy to install alternative operating systems, as I will describe in the advanced chapter.

If budget is an issue, consider purchasing a second-hand phone through sites such as eBay (**https://ebay.com**) and Swappa (**https://swappa.com**). Make sure any phone you buy second hand is not blacklisted (you can check using the tool at **https://swappa.com/esn**), and always put it through a full reset when you receive it. When you buy a phone, if at all possible make sure that it is unlocked, i.e. not tied to a particular cellular provider. Always buy a protective case that will keep your phone physically protected.

Choosing the best cellular service

Almost all of the cellular services in the U.S. are provided by one of three "top tier" companies: AT&T, Verizon and T-Mobile, which also acquired Sprint in early 2020. You can purchase cellular service directly from one of these companies, or from one of a large number of *Mobile Virtual Network Operator* (MVNOs), companies that resell service on one of the top three providers often at discounted prices. The main difference between service from a top-tier provider and an MVNO is that the top tier providers usually prioritize the MVNO lower than their own direct service, meaning that if you are using an MVNO in an area that has high usage, either routinely such as in a city, or where there is congestion due to an event such as a sports game or an emergency situation, then you could see your data speeds drop dramatically, or even lose service altogether. Cellular providers offer two kinds of billing for service: *postpaid* in which you are billed monthly for services used, sometimes with a commitment for a period of time, and *prepaid* in which you purchase service in advance, and do not have any ongoing commitment. There are many benefits to using prepaid service. For postpaid, you will likely have to provide all kinds of personal details when you sign up, including often giving your social security number and consenting to a credit check. For prepaid, there is no such requirement, and with some services you do not have to provide any personally identifying information at all. This is an incredibly important part of a digitally resilient strategy, because if you don't have to provide personal details to the cellphone company, it is much harder for the location information from your cellphone to be tied to you individually. Also, with prepaid, you do not run the risk of having the company incur extra charges or continuing to bill you when you try to stop service. For these reasons, I strongly recommend a prepaid service. The primary decision between top-tier and MVNO will be a balance of cost versus reliability, and this is something only you can decide. MVNOs that I have had good experience with include Simple Mobile (**https://www.simplemobile.com**) and Mint Mobile (**https://www.mintmobile.com**). Both are on the T-Mobile network.

Before making a decision on which service to choose, you should research the coverage, reliability and speed of the top-tier provider that your service uses. A good starting point for coverage is to inspect the published coverage maps from the providers. These are available directly from the websites of the top-tier providers: AT&T (**https://www.att.com/maps/wireless-coverage.html**), Verizon Wireless (**https://www.verizon.com/coverage-map**), and T-Mobile (https://www.t-mobile.com/coverage/coverage-map).

For speed and reliability, I recommend installing the OpenSignal application (**https://www.opensignal.com/apps**). OpenSignal collects signal strength and speed reports from many users, making these available on a map. If you are not comfortable sharing your location and signal information with OpenSignal, you can turn off sharing in the settings. On the Map tab, you will see reports in your area color-coded by coverage. If you touch the "View Network Stats" button, you are shown average speed reports from users in your area on different networks. The reports from my area are shown in Figure 4.1.

Operator	Download (Mbps)	Upload (Mbps)
AT&T	36.13	8.34
Sprint	33.39	2.72
T-Mobile	14.93	4.72
Verizon	23.73	5.53

Figure 4.1. Network statistics in the author's area from OpenSignal.

If you are using or planning to use an MVNO, your speed will likely not be reliably as fast as if you have service with a top-tier provider, and you may just need to do your own testing. I expect that performance will be similar among MVNOs that use the same top-tier provider, although it is possible that they are treated differentially. Some MVNOs such as Mint Mobile offer a free testing period (you just pay for the SIM). Be sure to do multiple tests as speed can vary greatly at different times and locations. For example, in my experiments with Simple Mobile and Mint Mobile, I have had speeds as low as 2mbps and as high as 40mbps in the same town a few minutes apart.

Those of you who are first responders in the U.S. should definitely consider FirstNet (**https://www.firstnet.com**). FirstNet is a high-reliability cellular network built by AT&T and funded by the government that is specifically for first responders. In particular, FirstNet is designed to still work even if consumer cellular networks are overloaded. First responders are eligible for FirstNet service, which includes unlimited calls, text and data for $30/month, but you do have to obtain this through your agency.

Overall, I recommend always using prepaid service and give as little information as possible. Based on your calculus of cost versus reliability, choose a plan either from a top-tier provider, or an MNVO. Do research to determine the best services in the areas in which you travel. If you are a first responder, FirstNet might be the best service for you, at least in terms of reliability.

Switching to Voice-over-IP

It is likely as your read this you are thinking that switching to a different service is difficult for you as you are tied to a particular plan, or you have a phone number that you don't want to lose. Here I will describe a strategy that will let you manage the transition away from your existing plan easily. The strategy is to move your existing cellphone number to a *Google Voice* Voice-over-IP (VoIP) number, obtain a new prepaid cellular service, and then either set up Google Voice on your phone, or create one or more brand new VoIP numbers to use as your primary number, and then set the Google Voice to forward to one of your new numbers.

Why would you want to do this? Well there are many reasons. Giving out your "real" cellphone number brings risks. The number will likely end up in online people-search databases, which means that anyone with a few hundred dollars can likely find out not just your cellphone number, but also your location history from cellphone provider records. Knowledge of your phone number makes you vulnerable to "SIM swapping" attacks in which malicious actors effectively steal your phone number and use it to intercept two-factor-authentication codes. Plus, as anyone who has tried to switch providers will attest, porting your phone number from one provider to another is usually something of a nightmare, so you become effectively tied indefinitely to one provider. The beauty of the strategy presented here is that you will never have to give out your "real" phone number – thus mitigating the vulnerabilities – and can change provider whenever you like, without having to take any action on your phone number at all.

Porting your phone number to Google Voice is relatively straight-forward and can usually be completed in a matter of hours. You will be charged a one-off $20 fee. Instructions can be found at **https://support.google.com/voice/answer/1065667**. If the port fails, it is usually because there is a mismatch with the name or address on file with your original provider. If you do have problems, Google support via the chat feature is very good. Once the number has ported successfully, you will be able to access your calls and text messages through your browser. You will not be able to access them on your phone yet, until you have activated new service.

Congratulations! You have now divorced your original phone number from your cellular service provider, and you can go ahead and cancel your existing cellular plan. Choose a new, prepaid service as described in the last section, which will usually involve purchasing a SIM starter pack from a store such as Best Buy. You will then need to create an account and activate the SIM online (for Mint Mobile, this is done through their phone app). You can pay for service either using prepaid service cards, or by giving a masked credit card (see last chapter). I recommend providing as little personal information as possible in this process. Once activation is complete, you will have a new cellphone number. Write this down, but remember you are never going to give this number to anyone, except perhaps Google, if you follow the first option below. Apart from 911 calls you will never need to make or receive calls on this number.

Once the service is set up, you have two options. The easiest is to keep using your original cellphone number by installing the Google Voice app on your phone to make and receive calls. The app will now be used in place of the phone and text messaging apps on your phone except for 911 calls which are not possible through Google Voice. This is a big improvement in smartphone resilience, as it means that you are no longer tied to a particular provider, you can make and receive phone calls when you do not have phone service and on multiple devices including your computer, and you are no longer giving out an identifier that can be used to track your location, at least for the future.

If you want to take things a step further, you might at this point consider one or more new phone numbers: the beauty of VoIP is that you can have as many as you like on one device. I am a big fan of the MySudo service (**https://mysudo.com**). MySudo is product of privacy-focused company Anonyome Labs that allows you to have up to 10 different identities, or "Sudos" operated from the same app. Each Sudo can have its own phone number and email address. This is an excellent way to compartmentalize – for example you can have one phone number for work, one for personal use, one for online shopping, and so on. Plans are available for the U.S. and Canada and phone numbers are available for the U.S., Canada and the U.K. In the U.S. prices start at 99¢ per month for one number. If you decide to go this route, you can still use the Google Voice app as described before for your "legacy" phone number, or you can set Google Voice to forward texts and voicemails to your email account, to ensure that you don't miss any calls from people without your new number.

Smartphone privacy & security settings

You can make big improvements to the privacy and security of your smartphone by changing some of your settings and implementing a few relatively easy behavior changes.

The first step is to make sure that your phone is protected with encryption and a secure password, just as you did for your computer in the first chapter. The good news is that on modern phones, encryption is enabled by default. If you have a recent iOS version (8 or later) or Android version (5 or later) and you have a passcode set, your phone should be encrypted. On Android you can check this by **Settings > Security**. Under "Encryption & credentials" it should state that your phone is encrypted. The PIN that you set should be at an absolute minimum 6 digits long, and if possible at least 10 digits. Since you probably use a fingerprint or FaceID to unlock your phone most of the time, having a long PIN number isn't as much of a burden as it used to be. There is a lot of discussion in security circles about whether you should use biometric authentication such as fingerprint or facial recognition, with the biggest concern being that while you can't be forced to remember your PIN number, you could be forced to push your finger on a pad or to have your face exposed to your phone. I personally am comfortable with using biometrics, but you should make your own decision on this.

The next big change for privacy is to minimize the extent to which your location is shared. There are several ways that your phone can reveal your location, the three main ways being the GPS device in your phone itself, cellphone tower triangulation (by monitoring your signal strength from multiple locations, the cellphone service provider can determine your location relatively accurately), and through detection of nearby devices of known location either via WiFi or Bluetooth. I recommend three steps to minimize the extent to which your location is shared with cellular service providers, cellphone operating system manufacturers such as Apple or Google, and other companies such as App providers:

1. Turn off Location Services in the phone settings entirely, except when you need it – such as when you are navigating to an unknown address. This will stop your phone sharing your location with apps on your phone or with the operating system manufacturers, except in some special cases such as if you make a 911 call. To turn off location services on iOS, go into **Settings > Privacy > Location Services**. On Android, go to **Settings > Location**.
2. Go into Airplane mode when you do not need cellular service. For example, when at home and on WiFi, you have no need for cellphone service if you are using a VoIP service for your phone calls. This will stop the cellular service provider from being able to deduce your location

through triangulation.
3. Turn off WiFi and Bluetooth when you are in dense environments, such as a shopping mall. This will prevent your WiFi and Bluetooth signals being used to identify your phone and thus location (this is a becoming a commonly-used technique to track you in stores).

The next change is to turn off cloud services, such as iCloud and Google Drive on your phone. My recommendation is that you turn off these services entirely, but again you should make your own decision on this. On iOS, go into Settings, and click on the bar at the top that shows your Apple ID. Tap on "iCloud", and then select which services you want to use iCloud for, or preferably turn them all off. On Android, go to **Settings > Google**, tap on your Google account, then on Account sync. Select which services you want to sync with Google (preferably none).

Next, let's review the permissions different apps can have. In iOS, this is in **Settings > Privacy**, and on Android it is in **Settings > Apps & notifications > App permissions (or Permission manager)**. On both operating systems, there is a list of categories of access, such as Microphone, Camera, and so on. Go through each of these and review which apps are given access. In particular, be particularly careful which apps have access to your location, camera and microphone. If in doubt, deny access – you can always turn it back on later.

I also recommend disabling voice command systems such as Siri, although you might find those services valuable. You should also ensure that your phone operating system is updated as soon as new versions are released. On iOS you can set updates to happen automatically in **Settings > General > Software Update > Automatic Updates**. On Android, go to **Settings > System** to see the options you have for automatic updates.

Smartphone backups & redundancy

What would be the consequence if your smartphone dies one day, or if it is stolen? If you implement the steps in this chapter to use VoIP and good security and privacy on your phone, the consequences should be fairly low, and you should be able to get a new phone set up quickly to make and receive calls on a new prepaid service if necessary. However, it can be useful to do a full backup of your phone, so that you don't lose anything.

Making a backup of an Apple iOS device is very easy if you have a MacOS computer too. Attach the phone to the computer using an appropriate cable (usually a Lightning-USB cable), and follow the prompts on the phone to confirm that the computer and phone can talk to each other (note that this will also mean that Apple knows that these two devices are related to each other). If you open up a Finder window, you should now see the phone listed in the panel on the left. Click on it, and then select "Back up all of the data on this iPhone to this Mac". This ensures that your backup is only kept on your computer, and is not uploaded to iCloud. Make sure "Encrypt local backup" is checked, and select a strong password. You can then click Back Up Now to back up your phone. If you ever need to restore, for example to a new device, simply follow the same process but instead click Restore Backup.

Unfortunately, there is no easy way to make a local backup of an Android phone. If you are comfortable uploading your phone data to Google, then you can make use of the Google backup feature. This is usually found in **Settings > Backup & reset > Back up my data**.

If you have a spare, old phone, you might consider setting it up as a backup phone in case your main phone dies or is lost. This will be a "Wi-Fi only" phone for now, but if you use VoIP this doesn't matter too much. You can either set up the old phone separately, or restore a backup of your main phone.

Apps for resiliency

There are now plenty of applications you can install on your smartphone that can help you not just be more digitally resilient, but also be more prepared and informed when the unexpected happens. Here are some of my favorite apps.

FEMA. This app from the Federal Emergency Management Agency will give you real-time alerts of emergency situations such as weather warnings in your area, as well as providing information on how you should respond to specific emergency situations. It is available on the App Store and Google Play store.

Firefox Focus. This is a minimalist browser that emphasizes privacy and security. It includes blocking of trackers and ads. Each time you use it you can erase the history, so you avoid websites tracking you across sessions and sites. Available on the App Store and Google Play store.

FM Radio. Some Android phones include a chip with a built-in FM radio. Check the apps that came bundled with your phone to see if there is an FM Radio app. It usually requires you to use plug-in headphones which double as an antenna. This can be useful, as it could provide you a way of getting information if the cellphone networks or the Internet were not accessible.

KeePassDX. This is an open source password manager for Android that is compatible with KeePassXC files. I prefer to always make changes to the password files on the computer, and just upload them to my phone for use. Available in the Google Play Store.

Lockdown Privacy. Lockdown Privacy is an app for iOS devices that blocks trackers and malware in your apps. It works by acting like a Virtual Private Network (VPN) for the phone, intercepting internet traffic from apps and blocking access to known trackers from companies like Google and Android. You can choose which kinds to block in the settings. Available on the App Store.

Magic Earth. This is a free maps and navigation app based on OpenStreetMap data that allows you to download maps for offline use, meaning you can still continue to navigate if you don't have an active Internet connection. Available on the App Store and Google Play store.

MySudo. As described above, MySudo is an app that allows you to create up to nine Voice-over-IP phone numbers, each of which is paired with an email address. Plans start at 99¢ per month for a single number. Available on the App Store and Google Play store.

OpenSignal. As described above, OpenSignal is an app that will test the Internet connection speed on your phone, as well as showing you information on the average speeds on different cellular providers. Available on the App Store and Google Play store.

OSMAnd. This is another free mapping and navigation app that allows download of maps for offline use. This app is more focused on hiking, walking and outdoor recreation than Magic Earth which is better at vehicle navigation. Available on the App Store and Google Play store.

Privacy. The app for the Privacy.com service allows you to manage virtual credit cards very easily. Available on the App Store and Google Play store.

ProtonVPN. The ProtonVPN app gives you access to the ProtonVPN Virtual Private Network service which masks your IP address. This can be useful particularly if you need to use a public WiFi connection. You can create a free account which is usually fast enough for use on a phone. Note that if you want to use this app along with the Lockdown app, you will have to select the IKEv2 protocol in the Settings. Available on the App Store and Google Play store.

Pulsepoint. This is a 911-connected mobile phone application that allows users to view and receive alerts on calls being responded to by fire departments and emergency medical services. It only is enabled in some areas of the U.S., so check that your area is covered. It is especially useful to receive notifications of traffic accidents and structure fires that could cause traffic backups. Available on the App Store and Google Play store.

Quakefeed. Quakefeed will give you notifications of earthquakes. You can set the criteria for the earthquakes that want to be notified about. This uses information from the US Geological Survey (note that this is different than the immediate notifications from the early warning system which can be found at **https://www.shakealert.org**). Available in the App Store and Google Play Store.

Radarscope. I believe Radarscope is the best available weather radar app, with coverage across the U.S. It is a rich information source if severe weather such as tornadoes and severe thunderstorms affect your area. The app includes information on current weather warnings. It is available for $9.99 from the App Store and Google Play store.

Scanner Radio Pro. This app allows to you listen to live audio from over 7,000 fire and police scanners, weather radios, amateur radio repeaters, air traffic and marine radios from around the world. This can give you useful information in the event of an emergency situation. The app uses the live feeds from **https://www.broadcastify.com** where you can check to see if your area is covered. A particularly useful feature is the "listener alerts" that notify you if a scanner suddenly gets lots of listeners, indicating a potential major event happening. Available on the App Store and Google Play store for $2.99.

Signal. Signal is a free secure and private messaging app that uses zero-knowledge end-to-end encryption. It is a much more secure and private way to communicate with people than standard SMS messaging, and it works any time you have an Internet connection. Available on the App Store and Google Play store.

Strongbox. This is a password manager app for iOS that is compatible with KeePassXC. If your phone and computer are on the same network, you can easily upload your password files to your phone by going to a local area IP address on your computer that links to your phone. I prefer to always make changes to the password files on the computer, and just upload them to my phone for use. Available in the App Store.

Zello. Zello is a two-way radio and messaging app that can be used to keep in touch with friends and family, and is particularly useful in an emergency situation as it requires low bandwidth to work. The app has been used in emergency situations such as hurricanes to help connect people who need help with those who can provide it. Available on the App Store and Google Play store.

Digitally resilient smartphone checklist

- [ ] Obtain unlocked, modern smartphone, preferably Apple or Google Pixel
- [ ] Identify the best top-tier service in your area and the areas to which you travel
- [ ] Select a prepaid service and purchase a SIM starter kit
- [ ] Port your existing number to Google Voice
- [ ] Activate new prepaid service on your phone
- [ ] Cancel your existing service
- [ ] Decide on VoIP strategy. Install Google Voice App, or forward calls from your old number and create new VoIP numbers, e.g. with MySudo
- [ ] Review privacy and security settings
- [ ] Consider changing usage of cellular service, WiFi and Bluetooth to minimize location sharing
- [ ] Decide on a backup strategy for your phone
- [ ] Decide if you wish to install any additional apps for resilience

Chapter Five

Advanced Digital Resilience

The previous chapters describe steps to improve digital resilience that apply to almost everyone. In this chapter, I will cover some special advanced digital resilience topics. Some of these are quite experimental, and others quite extreme, so you must make your own decisions about which, if any, are useful for you.

Threat Modeling

Most people are not very good at accurately assessing risk. We tend to spend time worrying about rare events out of our control, and neglect to prepare for much more likely threats that we can control, at least to some degree. Threat modeling is a process that is popular in the cybersecurity community for identifying and ranking specific threats. If you have implemented the steps laid out in the previous chapters, you have already made big mitigations of some of the most common threats such as losing your computer contents, or having your Internet accounts hacked. As an advanced digital resilience practitioner, you can use threat modeling to identify and prioritize special threats that you face, leading to ways that you can mitigate those threats.

There are several methods for implementing a threat model, but the one I think is most helpful here uses five questions:

1. What **assets** are you trying to protect?
2. What **threats** are you trying to protect your assets from?
3. What is the **probability** of the threat becoming real, and what would be the **impact**?
4. What **mitigations** could reduce the probabilities or impacts?
5. What **plans** should you put in place for if the threats become real?

The probability and impact can be assessed qualitatively (that is, in words), or numerically. Using numerical assessments allows you to compare threats with each other. A simple numerical scoring system for probability would be a score between 0 and 1 that represents the probability of an event happening in the next ten years; zero representing a certainty that it will not happen, and 1 a certainty that it will happen. Similarly, you can use a 0-1 scale for impact, for example:

1.0 Catastrophic – devastation, no recovery possible
0.9 Catastrophic – devastation, very difficult to recover from
0.8 Critical – serious, lasting damage requiring big changes to recover from
0.7 Critical – serious, lasting damage requiring moderate changes to recover from
0.6 High – very significant negative effects over years
0.5 High – very significant negative effects over weeks or significant effects over years

0.4 Moderate – significant negative effects over weeks or minor effects over years
0.3 Moderate – significant negative effects over days or minor effects over weeks
0.2 Low – minor negative effects but full recovery in hours or days, no lasting impact
0.1 Low – some minor negligible disruption but life continues as normal

With numeric probabilities and impacts, you can calculate a risk score, which is usually done by multiplying the probability by the impact. This results in a risk score between 0 and 1, where a 1 would represent a threat that is certain and catastrophic.

The questions can be answered for different threat scenarios, and at different times. For example, let's say you run a business that involves highly critical and confidential data that is stored on your laptop. Some of this data is also stored in OneDrive. If this data is compromised or lost, it could mean the end of your business, a lawsuit, or prosecution. Further, you believe that competitors or hackers may be trying to obtain this confidential information. At the current time, you are not making backups of the data on your laptop and your hard drive is encrypted but with a weak password. You might answer the first three questions as follows:

Asset	Threat	Probability	Impact	Risk
Confidential files stored on laptop computer	Accidental loss	0.3	0.7	0.21
	Hardware failure	0.2	0.7	0.14
	Theft of laptop	0.1	0.8	0.08
	OneDrive account hacked	0.1	0.8	0.08
	OneDrive account access lost	0.1	0.8	0.08

Accidental loss is thus ranked your highest risk, followed by hardware failure. You can then use this ranking to identify mitigations that would reduce either the impacts, probabilities, or both. For example, after implementing a strong password on your laptop, a secure backup strategy, and deleting your OneDrive account, your responses could change as follows:

Asset	Threat	Probability	Impact	Risk
Confidential files stored on laptop computer	Accidental loss	0.3	0.2	0.06
	Hardware failure	0.2	0.2	0.04
	Theft of laptop	0.1	0.3	0.03
	OneDrive account hacked	N/A	N/A	N/A
	OneDrive account access lost	N/A	N/A	N/A

The final step is to make plans for if a threat is realized, and if possible, test out these plans. For example, what would you do if your laptop is lost or has a hardware failure? Probably your plan would involve purchasing a new laptop, setting it up securely with encryption and a strong password, and restoring your files from your backups. The act of planning will reveal steps that you need to take now to ensure that the plan goes smoothly if needed. For example, do you need to start saving money for a new laptop now? How easy is it to retrieve your files from backup?

Using Linux and Free & Open-Source Software

Throughout this book, I have assumed that you are using either a Windows or MacOS computer. As I mentioned, there is a third option called Linux. Linux is an open-source operating system, meaning that it is maintained by a large group of volunteers, and all of the code for it is free and publicly available. This makes it more resilient than a closed-source operating system like MacOS or Windows, as your access to it is not dependent on the will of a single company, and if you wish you could even examine the code to see what it is doing. The first version of Linux was released in 1991 by Linus Torvalds. There are now many variants of Linux that you can download. Here I will focus on two: Ubuntu and Tails.

Ubuntu is one of the most popular versions, and the interface will be quite familiar to anyone who has used Windows or MacOS. The easiest way to start trying out Ubuntu is to download the ISO file for Ubuntu Desktop, and then install that onto a bootable USB flash drive, which you can then use to try out Ubuntu, and then install it if you wish. Here are the steps you need to take to try out Ubuntu:

1. Download Ubuntu Desktop from **https://ubuntu.com/download/desktop**. At the time of writing, the current version is 20.04.1 LTS.
2. Install Ubuntu on a USB flash drive, which must be 2GB or larger. Instructions for creating the bootable USB flash drive on Windows computers can be found at **https://ubuntu.com/tutorials/create-a-usb-stick-on-windows** and for MacOS computers at **https://ubuntu.com/tutorials/create-a-usb-stick-on-macos**.
3. Once you have created the bootable USB flash drive, you will need to reboot your computer and instruct it to boot off of the flash drive instead of the hard drive. On a Windows machine, you will need to reboot your computer and press a particular key as it reboots to access the Boot Menu. The exact key depends on the manufacturer, but is usually either Esc, F2, F10 or F12. You might just need to experiment, or look up the right key for your particular computer. Once successful, you should see a list of options for booting – choose the USB device and press Enter. On MacOS, insert the USB flash drive into a USB port (if you have a more recent MacBook you will need to use a USB-C to USB converter), choose Restart from the Apple Menu, then as the computer is rebooting hold down the Option key. You will then be shown a screen that lets you select which device to boot from – double click the USB device then wait for Ubuntu to boot. Note that it is OK to press Control-C to skip the disk check to speed up the boot.
4. You will then see a screen that allows you to "Try Ubuntu" or "Install Ubuntu". If you click Try Ubuntu, you will be able to use a fully functional Ubuntu instance that uses your computer RAM instead of the hard disk. This means that everything you do will be

lost when you turn off the computer, but it is a great way to try out Linux – and also can be used if you want to test something out without risking your permanent installation.

The Ubuntu desktop can be seen in Figure 5.1. You can explore it yourself, or follow the getting started guide at **https://help.ubuntu.com/stable/ubuntu-help/getting-started.html**.

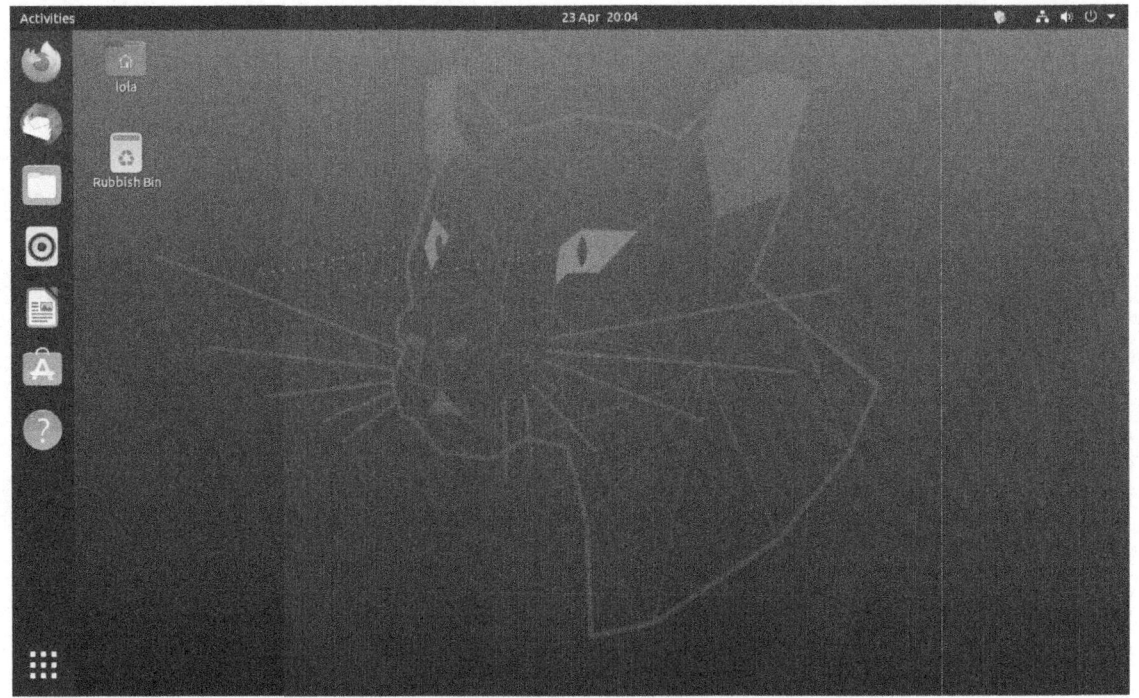

Figure 5.1. Ubuntu Desktop

There are a few ways in which using Linux is not as flexible as Windows or MacOS – the most apparent being that many commercial software packages do not work in Linux, most notably Microsoft Office products. However, there are many *Free & Open Source Software* (FOSS) products available for Linux, and you can explore these in the Ubuntu store. For example, LibreOffice is an open-source replacement for Microsoft Office.

If you decide you want to use Ubuntu as your primary operating system on one of your computers, the best way is to wipe the hard disk and replace it with Ubuntu, although it is possible to make a dual-boot machine. Detailed instructions for installing Ubuntu can be found at **https://ubuntu.com/tutorials/install-ubuntu-desktop**. In step 6, be sure to select "Encrypt the new Ubuntu installation for security" and select a strong password, which you will have to type in every time the computer boots up.

An alternate Linux variant is called Tails. Tails (**https://tails.boum.org**) has a strong focus on privacy and anonymity, with Internet connections forced to go through the Tor network (**https://www.torproject.org**), making it hard for your Internet usage to be tracked. It is especially useful when booted directly off a USB flash drive, as all local record of usage will then be erased when the machine is switched off. Tails is a particularly useful digital resilience strategy for those with extreme privacy and security needs, such as journalists or dissidents in repressive regimes. However, the Tor network is very slow, so it is not ideal for everyday use.

Of course, you don't have to install Linux to use Free and Open Source Software; there is plenty available for Windows and MacOS. FOSS is also available for Android devices through the F-droid store. You can download the F-droid app at **https://f-droid.org** and search it just like the Google Play store.

An open-source smartphone with GrapheneOS

As I mentioned in the smartphone chapter, you mostly have to buy into an Apple or Google ecosystem to use a smartphone. However, this is not entirely true. Since Android is an open source operating system, it is possible to adapt the code to "de-Google" it, removing the ties directly into the Google ecosystem. There are three main "branches" of Android which are de-Googled. Two of these, GrapheneOS (**https://grapheneos.org**) and CalyxOS (**https://calyxos.org**) are designed specifically for the Google Pixel phones. LineageOS (**https://lineageos.org**) will work on other brands of phone, but does not have as good security. In a similar way to a computer, using an open source, non-proprietary operating system can increase your digital resilience by reducing your dependence on big companies (i.e. giving more control), and removing the sharing of data with these companies.

My own preferred option is GrapheneOS, which is specially hardened for security, although CalyxOS is very similar and a good alternative. Both work on the Google Pixel range of phones, which were designed by Google with a very "open" architecture meaning it is possible to implement secure, alternative operating systems on them. If you would like to try GrapheneOS or CalyxOS, the installation process is similar for both, and involves downloading an installation file and "flashing" it to your phone. Instructions for GrapheneOS are at **https://grapheneos.org/install** and for CalyxOS at **https://calyxos.org/installation**.

Since your phone is now "de-Googled", you won't have access to the Google Play store, nor Google Play services that are required for some apps to work – although you do have the option with CalyxOS to install microG, which is an open source version of the Google services (but which does tie your phone back somewhat to Google). Instead of the Google Play Store, you can download the F-droid app (**https://f-droid.org**) which gives access to a wealth of open source applications, and the Aurora Store (**http://auroraoss.com/app_info.php?app_id=1**) which gives access to apps in the Google Play store without requiring a Google account.

Be aware that operating systems such as these are still somewhat experimental. Some apps will just not work, and others will only work partially, particularly those that require Google services.

Currently the MySudo VoIP app does not work on these operating systems, and several other apps will work but will not be able to use notifications properly, as these often require Google services.

Off-grid communications

How do you communicate with your co-workers, neighbors and friends? The chances are that even for people in the next office or the apartment next door, you currently communicate with them through an Internet-based service such as email or a social media app. Such communication requires a multi-layered stack of technologies to work properly that might be spread around the world. The message from you to your neighbor in New York might be sent via a server in Ireland using software maintained in India by a company based in San Francisco. There are thus multiple opportunities for failure, as well as for privacy or security lapses. Additionally, if your means of getting information is entirely dependent on the Internet, then if there is an infrastructure failure you may not be able to get important safety information in an emergency. Others may need to travel or live in places where access to the Internet or cellular networks is unreliable or non-existent.

An advanced digital resilience strategy should therefore include some consideration of *off-grid communications* – that is, ways to communicate that are not critically dependent on someone else's infrastructure. There are several ways of practicing off-grid communications, from well-established ones such as amateur radio, through to emerging technologies such as mesh networks. Here are some of the more practically useful ones.

Amateur radio. Portions of the radio spectrum in most frequency bands (shortwave, VHF, and so on) are set aside for use by amateur radio, sometimes called ham radio. With a long tradition in hobby radio, citizens around the world can, after passing a short technical exam, obtain an amateur radio license and callsign that permits them to broadcast on these frequencies, within certain rules. Amateur radio has been used since the earliest days in emergencies, due to the infrastructure-independent nature of the communications and the fact that radio hobbyists can often creatively rework equipment to fit the needs of a particular disaster. With the basic Technician license, you will be able to use VHF and UHF two-way radios that with the right antennas can communicate over several miles. With a General license, you will be able to use shortwave (HF) radio, which given the right atmospheric conditions can communicate between continents. Local amateur radio groups often actively experiment in the use of two-way radio for off-grid communications, and participate in emergency support functions. To learn more about amateur radio, go to http://www.arrl.org/what-is-ham-radio.

Personal two-way radios. Most countries set aside some radio frequencies, usually in the VHF or UHF areas of the spectrum, for unlicensed "personal use" (i.e. for families to keep in touch with each other over short distances). In the U.S., the best-known radio service is the Family Radio Service (FRS), which consists of 22 UHF frequencies designated for low power unlicensed use. Most "bubble-pack" radios sold in retail stores work on these frequencies. These radios are much more limited than commercial or amateur radios, but they can still provide a useful alternate short range (usually a mile or less) communications strategy, for instance with your neighbors. Canada has a license-free service that uses the same frequencies. In Europe, and a variety of other countries, the PMR446 service is a license free set of frequencies in the UHF band, similar to FRS in the U.S., but with 8 frequencies. Similar bubble-pack radios are sold in stores in these countries.

AM/FM radio. One of the cheapest and most useful pieces of off-grid communications technology you can invest in is a regular AM/FM radio. Some smartphones even have one built in. Should there be an infrastructure failure, an AM/FM radio might be the only source of emergency information that you have. In the U.S., there is a set of commercial radio stations called PEP (Primary Entry Point) stations, usually in the medium wave (AM) band, that are battle-hardened and serve as initial entry points for national *Emergency Alert System* traffic. In a widespread disaster situation, they could be vital information sources if local infrastructure is down. Coverage of PEP radio stations is shown in Figure 4.2 – you can look up the frequency of your nearest PEP station on the web. For instance, my nearest station is WLW Cincinnati (**https://en.wikipedia.org/wiki/WLW**) on 700kHz.

Figure 4.2 Coverage of Primary Entry Point (PEP) AM/FM radio stations in the U.S. A high-resolution version is available on mydigitalresilience.com. Map provided by Al Kenyon at FEMA.

Weather radios. In the United States, a network of VHF radio stations operated by the National Weather Service broadcast weather information and warnings 24 hours a day. Each of these stations operate on one of seven VHF radio frequencies (162.400, 162.425, 162.450, 162.475,

162.500, 162.525, 162.550). You can purchase weather radios that not only will receive these frequencies, but will sound an alert when a weather or other warning has been issued. A system called SAME (Specific Area Message Encoding) uses digital codes to identify warnings based on their location (by county), and nature. Recently other kinds of warnings have been added to the list, so weather radios are really becoming all hazards alert radios. The National Weather Service NOAA Weather Radio All Hazards site (**https://www.weather.gov/nwr**) gives much more information, including locations and frequencies of sites, and SAME codes for counties. It's worth noting that weather radios vary greatly in the amount of flexibility they offer – some will alert for all warnings, some you can specify that you only want to hear alarms for certain warnings in certain counties (e.g. tornado warnings). The Midland WR-400 is a good example of a weather radio offering this flexibility.

Public safety radio scanners. A variety of radio scanners are available that can receive transmissions from local police, fire, ambulance, and other responders. This can be a valuable source of information during an emergency situation. Scanners are available as handheld units that run off batteries meaning they can be taken anywhere; mobile units designed for installation in a vehicle or desktop use; and some hybrids such as the Uniden Home Patrol. Information on frequencies and kinds of systems used in the US and some other countries, broken down by state and county for the U.S., can be found on RadioReference (**https://radioreference.com**).

Mesh networks. A mesh network is a set of devices that organically form an extendable network by relaying messages for each other. They thus offer the possibility of taking a technology which is inherently short range, such as Bluetooth or low power radio communications, and using it to communicate over a much wider area via intermediate nodes. The simplest way to try a mesh network is using a mesh networking app on a smartphone that uses Bluetooth or WiFi to create an ad-hoc mesh network. Two popular mesh networking apps are Briar (**https://briarproject.org**) and Bridgefy (**https://bridgefy.me**). Bluetooth and WiFi are however very short range, so these apps really only work when there is a high density of people using the app. A neat solution is the GoTenna Mesh (**https://gotennamesh.com**), which connects to your phone by Bluetooth but which creates a mesh network using longer-range 900MHz frequencies. Mesh nodes can even be used as standalone repeaters, so it is even possible to provide city-wide coverage with some Mesh nodes on tall buildings (see for example **https://gotennamesh.com/blogs/ambassador-program**).

Knowledge Reboot Kits

In Chapter 2, I lay out a strategy for backing up your personal files, photos and email. But what about all the other information that you need at your fingertips? We take for granted that we can search for something on Google, navigate on a digital map, or access our favorite websites. What would happen if that access went away, either because we personally lose access to the Internet, or in the event of a widespread infrastructure failure?

Knowledge Reboot Kits (KRKs) are a way to cache important information offline so that it can be accessed without an Internet connection. There are many ways to make a KRK, but it can be as simple as purchasing an SSD drive and saving onto it copies of websites or other digital resources saved as local files. Firefox enables you to save a "complete web page" (**File > Save Page As**), which saves an HTML file for the page, along with a folder that contains embedded files such as images, meaning you can double click the HTML file and see the complete web page offline. In addition to web pages, you might consider including books (Project Gutenberg has a large selection of downloadable, free books **http://www.gutenberg.org**), PDF guides, manuals, and so on.

Kiwix (**https://www.kiwix.org**) is an open-source software project that allows you to store the entirety of Wikipedia, or any website locally on a computer or even a phone. Figure 4.3 shows a *Kiwix Hotspot* that I put onto a Raspberry Pi device (a small Linux computer) with a 128GB SD card for storage, which when powered up creates a WiFi hotspot that gives immediate access to the whole of Wikipedia. Kiwix can also be used to give access to Project Gutenberg, TED talks and other content.

Figure 4.3. Kiwix Hotspot that gives offline access to Wikipedia. The device is just 2.5" by 1".

Deleting your digital trail

Huge amounts of data is being collected about us all on a minute-by-minute basis. If you doubt this, simply search for your own name and address on one of the people-search sites such as BeenVerified (**https://www.beenverified.com**) or Intelius (**https://www.intelius.com**) to see how much information is available publicly. This likely includes your name, address, age, perhaps your employer and approximate salary, and with a few dollars you can likely purchase information on criminal records and so on. This is just the tip of the iceberg – much more detailed data and analytics about you is owned and shared by companies with each other.

This "digital trail" that you are producing might not bother you, but for some people such as those fleeing abusive spouses it can be a matter of life and death. For those that have a critical need or interest in removing their visibility on the web and elsewhere entirely, I strongly recommend Michael Bazzell's book *Extreme Privacy: What it takes to Disappear Second Edition*, available on Amazon (**https://inteltechniques.com/book7.html**).

I have already discussed some steps that will reduce your digital trail. There are a few additional steps I would recommend for any advanced digital resilience practitioner. The first is, when creating new Internet accounts, give as little personally-identifiable information as possible. For example, let's say a slightly sketchy web service that you need to use asks for a username, name, password, address, phone number, credit card number. Instead of giving away my personal information, I could do the following:

- *Username*: use something entirely made-up that you keep in your password manager, such as "wfzgoobah"
- *Name*: use an alias name, such as "Jenny Person"
- *Password*: secure password created by password manager
- *Address*: I will discuss address strategies below
- *Phone number*: have a VoIP number dedicated to sketchy websites
- *Credit card number*: use a masked credit card with Privacy.com

For addresses in the U.S., if you need to give a valid address but are not actually likely to need to receive anything there, the post office offers a "general delivery" service at most post offices that allows you to use an address of "GENERAL DELIVERY, Town, State, XXXXX-9999" where XXXXX is the ZIP code of the post office (**https://faq.usps.com/s/article/What-is-General-Delivery**). You will have to show ID to pick up mail. For instances where you need to actually receive mail or packages, there are two options that will provide some privacy. I strongly recommend obtaining a P.O. Box at the post office, or a similar service at a commercial mail receiving agency such as UPS. This will give you an address where you can receive mail, but which doesn't reveal your home address. Most post offices allow you to use the street address of the post office, with the PO box number included as if it were an apartment number. If you want to receive mail at your home address, consider using an "alias name". The first time you do this, the person delivering your mail might question whether the package is meant for you, but they will soon get used to it. This will mean that data mining companies will get your address, but associated with a different name.

I should make a comment about the use of alias names. I am not a lawyer, so if in any doubt ask a real lawyer. But my understanding is that it is acceptable to use a different name than your legal name for many things, so long as you are not stealing someone else's identity, and are not using it to commit fraud. The exceptions to this in the U.S. are you must always give your real name to any government official, such as a police officer or social security clerk, or to financial institutions, such as a bank.

The second recommendation is that you take some time to opt out of the most common people search sites on the web. If you do this, it will be a bit harder for people to find your real personal details with a quick Google search. Michael Bazzell has created a useful workbook for this (**https://inteltechniques.com/data/workbook.pdf**).

Chapter Six

Conclusion

In this book, I present a practical set of steps to make your computer, smartphone and Internet usage digitally resilient, with a robust backup system for your important files, and introduce some advanced techniques for those who want to take things a step further. As you implement these steps, I encourage you to make digital resilience a routine part of your approach to adoption of any new technology, be it a new washing machine or car, or signing up for a new Internet service. In particular, consider the four foundational concepts:

- Reliability and redundancy. How easily could this technology go wrong, and what is the backup if it does go wrong? What are the consequences of failure?
- Security. How can I keep strong security so that the device, or my data stored in the device or service, has a low risk of being stolen or exposed?
- Privacy. What will be done with my personal information related to this technology? What could be the consequences of it getting into the wrong hands? How do I minimize the amount of private information I provide?
- Control. How much can I control what this technology does and how it works? Can I repair it if it goes wrong? What are its critical dependencies, such as power, Internet access, or servers in other locations? How can I increase local control?

I hope you have enjoyed taking this journey into digital resilience, and that you feel reassured that your use of tech is now more reliable, secure, private and under your control. You have now taken some big steps towards being digitally resilient.

Made in the USA
Middletown, DE
04 April 2023

27701813R00040